Books by Stark Young

THE PAVILION

IMMORTAL SHADOWS

FELICIANA

SO RED THE ROSE

THE STREET OF THE ISLANDS

RIVER HOUSE

THE TORCHES FLARE

HEAVEN TREES

GLAMOUR

THE THREE FOUNTAINS

THE FLOWER IN DRAMA

The Flower in Drama

AND

Glamour

The Flower in DRAMA

&

GLAMOUR

THEATRE ESSAYS
and CRITICISM

by STARK YOUNG

REVISED EDITION

Charles Scribner's Sons

NEW YORK 1955

For permission to reprint parts of this volume I am indebted to the editors of *The New Republic* and *Theatre Arts Magazine*.

S. Y.

If one aims only at the beautiful, the flower is sure to appear.   SEAMI (1363–1444)

CONTENTS

CONTENTS

The Flower in Drama

AND

Glamour

ACTING

THE old and endless discussions as to whether acting is an art or not are useful in so far as they describe acting and make its principles more luminous. Every art is a form of translation by which one thing is expressed in terms of another, and, as Plato says, something then appears that was not there before. Acting is a business of translating into the terms of human beings certain matter taken either from life direct or from drama of thought and action that has been created out of life. The completeness of acting as art depends on the completeness of the translation it makes into its own terms.

If you wish to discuss acting as an art with any fundamental point, you have to reach into the air almost and pull down your own matter. On the subject in general little has been written. And the criticism of actors is usually not about acting at all, but a matter of mere impression and mutual personalities. And many even of the best and most inspired lovers of the theatre do not think of acting fundamentally. What they look for in acting is a thrill. They look for the consummate and exciting pleasure that may come

3

from some radiant being there on the stage. They
mean by acting a kind of magnetism that stirs
them coming from some luminous body. They
mean personal distinction. They mean a human
quality that is transcendent and that seems in
itself creative. But the point is that this wonderful
and radiant person is not a figure in the art of
acting only. Such distinction counts more immediately in acting than in any other art, because
the medium employed is the actor's presence.
But such people are not confined to acting; they
occur in every art. This supreme quality in this
radiant individual is not the art of acting. It is
a material for that art. In acting, the personal
quality of the actor is a part of the material that
the art works in, precisely as is a voice, or a hand,
or a mind.

What such lovers of the theatre need to remember is that acting is first a craft. To forget
that fact is to look for the thrill of towers or
the magic of light on windows and to ignore con-
struction and architecture. To talk of flashes of
inspiration and thrills and devastating magnetism is not to discuss acting, but only certain
heavenly by-products of the art. As in architecture or any other art, acting has an honest ground-
work of essentials and certain hard fundamentals
on which it stands. There is much in it that merely
clears the way, supplies the vehicle for any fine
quality that may come along. If he has no dis-

tinction of his own, a man may, in a sense, be an actor and not an artist at all. And a man of the most radiant distinction, if he lacks grounding in these essentials of acting, may be by temperament an artist but not yet an actor. These essentials of the art remain the same, from the humblest craftsman to the most magnificent figure in the theatre anywhere; and they are the basis of an art of acting. All sorts of methods and theories and dominant or superb personalities may arise, but the fundamentals of the art as an art do not change. All art, translating into its own terms and adding something that was not there before, is like the human body, which translates into itself a certain matter and adds vitality. An art of living, no matter how attractive, must first of all be founded on the nature of the body. An art of acting must be founded on the nature of acting's fundamentals. These remain themselves; and are only dilated and perfected by the changes, physical and spiritual, that arise.

But acting shares with religion and literature the disadvantage of every one's expertness on the subject. When people are ill they send for a doctor; when they see paintings they consider professional judgments; and when their switchboards fail they call the electrician. But, exactly as he is confident of his religion and of what a good story must be, every one knows that he knows good acting when he sees it. And in the life of the theatre, acting is the closest of all things to the common man. Acting is what he looks at in the theatre always, even the poor acting that he often sees, rather than at anything else. However much visionaries and reformers in the theatre may have pushed the accent toward lighting and scenery, *décor*, music, and design, the common man stays by the actors. He knows that what makes the whole thing alive to him and makes it theatre is the presence of those men and women on the stage who bring the whole affair to life before his eyes. And so he concludes, then, that he can see acting, just as he believes that he sees religion and literature, or as he believes that he sees the world about him, though he may not even see that the color of shadows in the morning differs from their colors after noon. But whatever he may think, he is far from expert. Without practice or familiarity or study the average man knows no more about acting than he does about architecture or music. He may respond to acting in a manner very different from his response to music or architecture, but that proves nothing. You may as well say that his response to a caress proves that he knows biology. For acting, all the methods necessary for learning to read a language, for judging a literature are needed.

One must have seen it often and intelligently, have endured boredom and ecstasy, have made comparisons through experience and repetition, have formed in one's mind ideals and models of what one thinks admirable.

This habit that the average man indulges of being, where acting is concerned, so much at home in Zion leads him to conclude that actors must become each of the parts assumed. All the actors have to do, he thinks, is to take whatever characters fall to them and reproduce them as they are in life. He concludes that the purpose of acting is to reproduce reality so exactly that we might easily mistake one for the other. The highest compliment that most people can pay an actor takes this line. Chaliapin does not act Boris, they will say, Chaliapin *is* Boris. But what Boris they mean, or who Boris was, they do not say, or whether they have seen his likeness or read his journals.

The desire for illusion in acting is a childish weakness. One can understand it humanly; but after all it is too much like a monkey's delight in front of a mirror. Deception as an end in art brings us to nonsense. And from the confusion on this point acting suffers more than any other art; for this mania that people have, to find in art the illusion of the actual, pursues the actor to the last ditch. Many people who have got over thinking that the painting is art in which ears of corn are rendered so that under a strong light you cannot tell them from real corn, and who know that the rumbling at the bottom and tweedling at the top of the piano to reproduce the thunder and the shepherd's bells is not music, know nothing like that when it comes to acting. They think that an actor's greatest triumph consists in making us think him some other person than himself. They prefer sometimes when he has died on the stage to have an actor remain out of sight and not return to bow before them with a smile on his face. People who insist on such deception and identity should frequent the dog and pony show. There they would see perfect naturalness, perfect illusion. Rover does not indeed act dog. He *is* dog. It is by just this exactly that such critics of acting show what mere babies they are so far as art goes. For they would substitute the make-believe of children for that more difficult and final business of acting, which is the translating of its matter into another kind of truth.

This perplexity over the matter of illusion in acting has led to widely diverse theories of its purpose. At one extreme we have what is called representational acting, at the other, presentational. The theory of representational acting, stated extremely, implies that the actor creates as completely as he can the illusion of a life going on which is apart from the audience,

but which the audience is allowed to look at.
The actor is not supposed to take the audience
into consideration, but to live the life of the
character he enacts quite as if the fourth wall
of the room he occupies had never been removed. The theory of presentational acting implies that the actor takes to the audience what
he has to act and shares the idea of it with
them. In the resulting creation that he achieves
the audience has a definite part. Grasso, for
example, when he does a death scene would
as soon present it on the floor of the foyer.
What he aims at is the presentation of the
idea of death and its struggle. He strives to
free and convey it to us very much as it
might be expressed in music. And music implies a listener. But, though these two theories
and kinds of acting may vary so widely, that
fact does not in the least unsettle the place in
it that illusion occupies. It is obvious that,
fourth wall or no, our understanding of a rôle
depends on what the actor chooses to set forth
in it, and our pleasure depends on our knowing
that it is art, not life, we are looking at. It is
obvious that resemblance, make-up, impersonation become important according to the amount
in them of choice, of design, of idea. When
acting carries us out of ourselves it is not that
we are deceived by what we see; we are swept
by the power of the actor's idea; it is not so

much some one's actually dying that we weep over; we weep over the agony of death. One often hears people say that the illusion in some scene was so perfect that they were carried entirely out of themselves. In a torture scene, for example, acted by Réjane, one might get so strong a sense of reality as to be made sick by it. But what makes us sick is not that we think some one is really being tortured, but rather that the sense of suffering and strain is made so powerful and so compelling that we are overcome by it. Réjane does not fool us so much as she dominates our state of mind. In sum it is obvious that if a thing is life, then it is not art. Acting is not art until it ceases to be life. It is not art until it takes what it portrays and recreates that in its own terms and adds to it something that was not there before.

The problem of acting is how to find in its actual material the significant pattern or result. It has, therefore, essentially the same problem as painting has or sculpture; but in some ways its problem is more difficult. The painter or the sculptor has to struggle with a different kind of immediacy in his material. The mere actuality need not get so much in his way. He may abandon more easily all reproduction of the actual object if he likes, and make a piece of pure design. But the actor has to deal with a more intractable reality in the shape of his own person and the other actors, and the problem of achieving a fine translation of this reality into his art is his last and profoundest issue.

People may go on saying till doomsday that this disguise of himself, this reproduction of actual persons, is what they judge an actor by. But their experience and their preference in actors do not bear this out. Great actors remain themselves. Duse, Bernhardt, Chaliapin, Grasso, Nijinsky are always themselves under their various parts. And Charlie Chaplin, who never loses his identity for a moment, is the best known and final proof of this point.

It is commonly declared that an artist like Guitry, or Novelli, is different in every part, and in every part is the very man portrayed. But the truth is that these actors are always themselves. It is only by an effort that they are able to become even in terms of themselves another character. In acting, as in sculpture or any other art, the medium resists the idea. What we get as a delineation is the result of the struggle of the actor's self with the self he tries to force upon it. It is the power of these great actors' conception and their ability to create this conception in terms of themselves that convinces us of the exactitude of each part. These actors in themselves supply a sort of continuity of radiance that shines through and illuminates and makes visible the quality of the characters they assume.

Actors remain artists, therefore, in proportion to the extent to which they remain themselves and translate into the terms of themselves the thing to be created. They are firmly fixed at the centre. They remain themselves, even though it may not be their immediate selves. And so it follows that their art depends wholly on what these selves of theirs profoundly are. The greatness of a man's acting will depend on the extent to which the elements of life may be gathered up in him for the spring toward luminous revelation, toward more abundant life. Art is a perpetual growth of life in other terms than itself. And the individual quality of the actor must always determine the quality of the terms in which his particular art expresses life. That the sensibility and intelligence—to use the old terms—of an actor, his gift, his soul, his music, his miracle of talent, are what measures his achievement, is indisputable. And though these may be partly born and partly acquired, they can never be overlooked or taken for granted. If you amount to nothing, your art in the end amounts to nothing; that is a fact almost biological in its brutal certainty. The actor's business is to remain himself forever; but to cause to grow in himself such flexibility and fluidity and eloquent magnetism of body, and such sympathy of the imagination, as may be translated into compelling presentations of human character and living. Only through this translation of the given character into himself can an actor profess to be an artist at all and the "lord of another's soul."

But no matter how great this self of the actor's may be, he cannot express it until he develops an adequate technic. Too many people on the stage have an easy belief that almost any one can act if he feels the emotion of the part in him and the will to do it. This is the volition theory, strong among earnest thinkers, Puritans and others, who have little knowledge of art, and like, in general, to believe that what you desire deeply enough you can achieve without the physical necessity of having a mind or skill. But will alone has obviously nothing in it but will. The will theory makes nonsense when you come to art, and drools all intelligence and point away into sleepy doxologies. Nature was never art; and merely feeling the rôle will never enable the actor to act, however delightful and democratic a state of affairs that might imply. An actor who has not found for himself technical machinery, one way or another, is like a man without a tongue; he may make all manner of sounds but never mean for other men what he has within him to say.

For how, without technic, shall the actor know
a way to discover out of many possible devices
and symbols those suited to his own physical
case and at the same time intelligible to men
in general? How, without technic, shall he be
sure of his voice, the most moving part of him?
How shall he know to regulate the tone, to
darken or whiten it; how know the retardation
and acceleration of rhythm; the actual speed
in relation to the effect of speed that is pro-
duced; the resistant flexibility, as Lewes called
it, that is the soul of elocution? How, if he
has not studied music or is at least musical by
nature, shall the actor maintain a rhythm, not
only in his speech but in his movements; how
shall he give to the very lines of his presence
on the stage a flow and unity, a continuous
design? How shall he know the difference between poverty and economy in his art; how
find in his material the elements at once real
and essential? Some effect an actor may get
by inspiration, if you like; by rising to some
emotion that possesses him. But how, without
technic, can he reduce what may be finely inspired but is incoherent to permanent and re-
liable comprehensibility. How can he fertilize
his mind as the field for inspiration? How,
without technic, shall he have the means to
accomplish what is the final test of acting: that
sound gradation of expression throughout a

whole piece? How shall he, in sum, be able to last through an entire part, and maintain a hardness of fibre that will not give out before the end is reached and the whole pattern exhibited? And even with all these, how can the actor be sure of his ability to repeat this achievement, as he must do, night after night? Without technic and practice, alas, these problems of his art will not only remain unmastered but will not even trouble him as necessary, if indeed they occur to him at all.

The actor, taking up a part, must have first of all an idea.

Before he can do anything with a part the actor, besides his feeling and his will to express it, and in addition also to his technical equipment, must have some idea in his mind, as Garrick told Diderot; some Homeric phantom, as Diderot put it, to which his mind can rise and with which he can identify himself. He can never play from nature direct, but from some idea—set up out of nature, if you like— in his mind. The actor plays from some imaginary being who is not his own self nor yet any self in nature. Homer, deserving to be praised for many other things, Aristotle says, is most to be praised because he knows what part to take himself. It is through his idea that the actor gets the rôle at the right distance from himself and in the right relation to himself.

A part of this conception and right relationship consists in an ability to perceive the quality of the thing acted, to perceive its school, its genre, its characteristic necessity—the ability, in sum, to act it in its own kind. The acting for Sheridan is as different from the acting for *The First Year* as the drawings in the *Saturday Evening Post* are from Sir Peter Lely, or as Beau Brummel's red heels from a pair of sport shoes, or a sedan chair from a hammock. The acting for Racine has little in common technically with the acting of Shakespeare. The characteristic quality must be translated into the acting or the whole performance will be pretty much rubbish. Without technic and culture the liveliest feeling and warmest enthusiasm in the world cannot discern or express those various qualities in drama, each with technical elements that are its own.

In the absence of skill among actors the softest way for the producer, the ordinary playwright and the audience is often to put actors in parts for which they are fitted congenitally, photographically; to find a blue-eyed boy for the blue-eyed rôle, sweets for the sweet, and fat to the fat. But this spoils acting as an art. It crosscuts to the merely expedient. The mere superficiality of likeness in an actor to a character will often satisfy and so evade the need of creating a piece of art. And through this he is led to omit the necessary exercise in creation and the constant practice in technic that can make him an artist. There have, obviously, been great actors who have been capable of only one kind of rôle, of one line; but it has always been at their peril as artists. It has never, moreover, been on a merely expedient and actualistic basis. These actors are always somewhat more than the line they take, the part they play; and they are not primarily related to it by their waist-line, their age, youth, or the length of their noses. For the artist on the stage, as Aristotle says of the poet, is not an imitator (mimetes), does not create an image, when he speaks himself.

The exercise of the imagination, the airing of our dreams, is one of the great pleasures of the theatre. If actors have no technic and no imagination, half our life in the theatre is left fallow in us; the poetic sides of the theatre remain unembodied. The keen use of the mind, the notes taken, the glancing recognitions of aptness in the actor's detail, is one of our delights. If actors have no acuteness, the prose portions of the theatre go stale and mediocre.

There is about the great acting of great moments in drama something that at once arouses and satisfies the imagination. It is a kind of inevitable revelation, a wide excitement that is due to the poignant identity of all the things involved. The recognition on our part of the relation between what is done and what is expressed is so luminous, so happy, so easy and complete, that it takes on the quality of inspiration. In *Mala Gloria*, for an illustration, the hero comes home from prison and a bandit's life to find that his wife has betrayed him for the young son of the house where she is employed as a maid. He kills her and departs again. What Grasso did when he acted the rôle was to kill the woman and then, instead of going straight out of the room, to turn on the young man, to turn madly, pause, catch his hand on the boy's head, kiss his brow suddenly, and spin him blindly from him; as you might treat a child who without knowing it has ruined your life. That was great imaginative acting; it left us with a sense of the entire content of the moment; it spread through infinite reaches of human significance.

But on a more familiar and less intense plane there is the satisfaction of sheer wit in the theatre. It is a quality less luminous than the finely imaginative; but it has, nevertheless, its own clarity and sharp eyes, it has aptness and that swift perception of neat similarities that we define as wit. Intense moments in the theatre, as in life, may without any comment supply their own imaginative depths. But the ordinary moments in drama are full of the ordinary elements of the familiar day. The pleasure we get from them comes from the liveliness with which we are able to perceive their contrasts and similarities and sharp, incongruous details. So that in this region of the familiar, if there is little technic and understanding on the actor's part, our loss is great, since at every moment the need appears for the sly philosophy and wit of the actors' own approach to his material. A great artist like Madame Yvette Guilbert—though she can have superb poetry at times—is, when she is at her prose best, a theatre of sheer mental exhilaration. Her perception and expression of the moment make an infectious riot in the mind and furnish a perpetual sense of quick cerebration, of epigram, of gay and easy precision. All impersonation—though it is a slow form of acting as a rule—depends for its success on its wit, which appears through the correspondence that we perceive between the acute observation of its subject-matter and the technic that conveys it. Apart from the greatest moments of drama and acting, this effect of wit and mental agility may be one of the theatre's greatest satisfactions. Acting may delight inexhaustibly by showing us how charming, how sane, how exciting, how satisfying sheer observation and economy may be.

If we have not expertness and distinction

among actors, audiences will no longer know what good acting is, except for the few simple human qualities so close to our natures that they act themselves. And audiences will have no way of learning what the nature of acting is; for, as with all arts, the only way to understand acting is by seeing it and being thrown with it. And where there is little art in acting, people come to look for what is called, for want of a better name, personality; they vaunt individuals, shout for one family of actors, follow one lady till her charms decline and then follow another. And the great distraction of the actor, his extreme craving for popularity—certainly natural enough in his case—becomes more and more purely personal, and on that account more precarious and often foolish. For, though the personal and individual appeal of an actor is basic so far as his art is concerned, the stressing of that appeal as mere personality is harmful for him as an artist and silly and stultifying for his admirers. All good actors are, through their technic and their distinction, comments on themselves and through themselves on the rôles they create. They speak as critics of life. When audiences forget to demand that comment and are willing to put up with the mere individual, acting sinks to journalism, to personal gossip, to a chatter of public privacies.

And worst of all, without capable actors dramatists forget what to write for. As artists, playwrights create in terms not of nature but of their art; and when the actors they see are unable to suggest anything but the mediocre or the merely accidental or incidental or personally good, these playwrights lose much of their inspiration. Not the ideal dramatist perhaps; his content may press to its own creation. But it is hard to picture even your great man as deeply urged to write for nincompoops who have no craft or range, or for talents that are wholly undeveloped and in a state of hit and miss. But for the lesser playwright the decline in his art may very well accompany the decline in the medium for its expression, the actor; and so we have a vicious circle, since the dramatists themselves have no little share in the state of acting that obtains.

It may be said of American acting at present that there is no way to tell just how much talent there is because of the lack of training by which that talent might be developed and exhibited. There are instances every season of beautiful acting, but there is no actor whose art may be said to be complete or transcendent. One thing our actors do well, the kind of thing that the English call very American. It is a certain effect of lively good nature, jazz, common sense, healthy spirits and energy. But this is a thin region after all, boyishly abundant on the prose side and covering a wide, but not very deep, section of our popular life. One would hate to think that such an art might represent what America most is. We have chiefly crowds of actors who never take the trouble to learn their business. The details of acting as a craft they pass by; they merely go on the stage. The unfortunate stage happens to be the direction in which egotism or opportunity leads them. They stand or fall by their own natural lustre. So far as one can tell, they do on the stage just what they would do off it; and we are supposed, perhaps, to think that merely seeing them there is delightful. But they have no technic either of manner, voice, diction, gesture, or of conception and projection in acting terms. It is often better to read the play than to see such actors stultify whatever life is in it. But acting with us is forwarded by the same methods as those on which razors and washing-powders rise to fame and automobiles become great. And a public without social cleavages or well-defined cultural criteria or authorities, follows whatever happens to be pushed to the front. On the Continent there are scores of persons who are favorites but are never mistaken for anything save what they are, mere amusers and popular pets. With us such persons are not only liked, they are acclaimed as celebrated

artists. And American audiences in their turn
have little to go by if they want to learn to
understand acting by seeing good examples of
it. Those who have not seen a dragon have
at least seen a great pinecone, Pausanias said,
trying to describe the scale corselets of certain
warriors. In our theatre we have few pine-
cones even to study the patterns of acting from.
For we lack the lesser type of actors, so common in Italy and France and Germany, in
whom we get technic, and sound technic at
that, without eminence. On the contrary, if
we have anything in America, it is more apt
to be the dragons, actors whom the vagaries of
talent alone have made significant. And this
is unfortunate. Such actors have nothing but
their own personal *flair* to shine with. Any
technical lessons that smaller or younger actors
could learn from them are worse than nothing;
imitators end by copying faults. And that only
sets us back; for it is better for acting in general
that we have bad imitations of good art than the
imitations of bad art that often succeed in New
York.

An Englishman who wishes to become an
actor starts off with handicaps in the very
medium of the art, in the means by which acting exists at all. He has an inexpressive body
to begin with. He instinctively mistrusts the
direct and free expression of emotion, and thus

he unconsciously shrinks the channels by which his inner life is released and the visible means by which it is conveyed to others. He lives in the midst of a society whose essential quality passes more easily into arts like literature and religion than into the art of the theatre. English acting has had great days no doubt and a lustre of shining names; but not now. English actors, when they do speak well, which is not always, speak better than ours do, though they have no standard of speech such as the French possess. They evince in their stage manner more security and poise than American actors do, and sometimes a certain kind of taste and restraint that is admirable. They enjoy a more solidly distributed method, a better gradation, than we do. And in social comedy they have a humorous and rich tradition, they have a droll analysis and intelligent irony where our actors are apt to have only vivacity, sentiment, and the sense of a joke. But in tragedy they lack flexibility in voice, gesture, and emotional current. And they have a way of substituting for passion and force and spiritual elegance a certain sweetish piety peculiarly their own and peculiarly false. And English actors have a way when they deal with a great classic of behaving as if it were the Bible; they display upon what they regard as classic a mistaken reverence and a sacred mannerism that throws the whole work out of joint. And, what is one of the most distressing limitations of all, both English and American actors suffer from that Anglo-Saxon trait so much indulged in the last century, the hatred of the premeditated in art. Because of this predeliction their acting gets into all sorts of foolish positions. Mentality, calculation, and arrangement are afraid of showing their heads. The idea of art as itself and as built up of its own designs is antagonistic to an Anglo-Saxon, who—though he knows in his heart that it is all bosh and that life and art both prove to the contrary—likes the effect of artlessness in art and of what he calls sincerity.

The German theatre is admirable first of all for its sense of ensemble, its reverence for the whole effect. German acting, moreover, does the folk thing well, the obstinacy of revolutionary motives, the vagaries of ordinary comedy. It has audacity, too, and this—though often unregulated by a finely civilized and urbane relaxation and choice—has given it a certain lead in the modern morbid and the bold ventures into new fields. German acting renders profoundly the turgid deep soul. But for idealities in the realm of acting, the great typical tragic emotion or the humorous ideality of farce, it falls short in style, in a spacious and open universality of emotion and form.

Style is what the French have over all other

stages, a sense of smart completion and taste and vivacious precision. And their greatest actors have style, also, in the greatest sense. In acting, as elsewhere, supreme style derives from a combination of sensibility and calculation, and moves toward the ideal of distinction with a touch in it of conscious elaboration or artifice. There is, of course, a vast amount of bad acting in France; but at its best French acting may easily be called the most discreet, the best regulated, the best placed of all. It exhibits not seldom a brilliantly observed propriety that might be said to affect one, as Henry James declared it affected him, as an almost celestial order. But it pays all too frequently for that kind of excellence. For this polish and effect of completeness French acting often pays in its imaginative limitations and in a sort of urban paucity of light and wings and devastating beauty of soul; it has the merits and the defects of its native genius.

Italian and Russian acting are beautiful in their naturalness. They evince the quality of naturalness in its most complete and inclusive sense. Both, according to the temperaments they express, are supremely free and natural in their use of an essentially artistic technic and endowment. Both have abundance, gusto, a passionate vitality, and soul. The Russian carries intensity farther in than the Italian

likes. His psychology is emotional and warm
and dark, where the Italian's is sharp and fiery
and clear and intellectualized. Russian and
Italian acting in the best examples have much
in common: a profound and exalted simplicity
in their truthfulness and realism, a magnificent
dignity and grave, warm beauty like nature's.
And Italian acting at its best, may, I think, be
said to excel the Russian only in one respect,
which, for want of a better phrase, I may call a
kind of civilized distinction. It has not only
the security and conviction of emotional power
and resource, but also an ease and a secure relaxation that rests on centuries of experience
and thought. The great faults of Italian acting are laziness, noise, and superfluous gesture,
the use of conventional theatre business to save
thought and labor. The same essential endowment for acting that makes the Italian achieve
supreme excellence in it, makes him capable of
the worst of the faults characteristic of this
particular art. No acting is worse than the
worst Italian. At its best Italian acting achieves
a beautiful suavity of method, a spontaniety,
a fluidity, and a fine relation between the inner
and outer parts of the human organism. Italian acting at its best has a kind of distinguished
actuality. It has the poetic realism that one
finds in early Renaissance marbles, the Guidarello Guidarelli at Ravenna, for example,

where the life within and the surface without seem to be one, and where nature in its outer representation is so exact, so delicate, so quivering and so exquisite that it is inseparable from the life within.

The actor's gift begins first of all with his body. In all countries and in all acting the measure of an actor's gift comes back to his body, comes back to the absorbing and revealing magnetism of his presence. His acting comes back to his body in the same sense exactly that all life, sensibility of perception and impression, and accuracy of general intelligence, come back to the body, to physical senses, to the earth. One of the first tests of an actor's talent is in the identity of his body and his mind. Not the actor's voice, not his brain, are the parts of him by which he becomes a medium for his art; it is his whole make-up, body, brain, and voice; it is the man you see before you on the stage. In fine acting the words and the body are at supreme moments inseparably one, and they can be said to be interchangeable in meaning and significance. It is not that the emotion is transferred from speech into a mimicry of gesture and facial play, not that—though the mere gift of miming need not be despised. It is that the idea that moves within becomes one with the outward form. The highest use of the body, of gesture, is not to reproduce, but to represent, with an added radiance, what is within, not, that is, to be an image but a symbol; the living content of the moment charges with its power the body that it animates, and makes it a symbol of its meaning. The idea that gathers up all its elements, the social, the ethical, the animal, into one thing in terms of the body, takes on magnificent power. The body, moreover, speaks to the eye, which is the door for so much of our experience. Gesture in some instances has a power beyond that of words, however splendid their golden eloquence may be. Gestures may give a concrete and arresting statement, a definite and convincing visual phenomenon that states the point as no words could ever do. The music of beautiful words spreads over and beyond the words themselves and their usual meaning into a beautiful immortality, into something less definite and more idea. And the flow of lines, the shifting emphasis of the actor's body, may weave an abstraction of design that has in it also some of the wider truth of music.

And acting itself is the body of the art of the theatre.

Acting has the same relation to the theatre that the body has to the expression of a man's life. And acting has the merits and the defects of the human being himself. Through its magnetism and its sensitive and expressive powers acting may serve to create the most beautiful ends, and even to carry the idea farther than the dramatist himself had ever conceived it. Or through laziness and egotism and stupidity acting may very well obstruct some great vision that from some great soul in the theatre arises. But it remains, nevertheless, the unescapable medium; and it can no more be kept out of account than the body can in the problem of one's living. Gordon Craig may wish to substitute marionettes for actors in the theatre; and Duse may say that to save the theatre we must first kill all the actors. But all this is only as great saints or fanatical dreamers in every century may have wished to rid themselves of the body, to stand free of the shackles of the flesh. And such a will as theirs, however haughtily it sets itself against the natural world that feeds and brings them up, has for certain spirits its shining fruits, even though when carried to its conclusion it is only a kind of divine nonsense, a mad symbol of beautiful desire. It is the dream of not existing in order to exist more completely. It is the nostalgia of the soul, solitary forever, for itself alone. It has something in it of that solemn verdict of those early fathers in Byzantium that the only salvation for the race of man was that no more children should be born into the world. And it represents a phenomenon that occurs in every art, the desire to escape from the art's medium. A simple pianist might wish the piano to sound like a harp. A visionary sculptor would like sculpture to be painting. A certain kind of poet wants poetry to be indistinguishable from music. And dreamers in the theatre move often toward some bastard or diverse art. But in the art of the theatre everything depends on two things: The first is the fundamental, natural base that nurtures it, which is the human quality of the actors. The second is the progression and sublimation of this fundamental material in the direction of idea. In the theatre, as in all life, vitality is sustained through a perpetual struggle of matter and idea and the eternal and delicately changing balance between them.

That acting, like religion and literature, should be felt as common knowledge among so many men who are by no means expert in them, is a disadvantage to its clarity and to the security of its theory and outline. Acting suffers through a closeness to life that makes it seemingly as an art or science more negligible than some arts appear to be. We forget with too much ease the delicacy and the security necessary to separate acting from life and make it an art. But as with religion and literature, this very closeness to life is acting's greatest asset, the evidence of its human immediacy and of the direct instinct with which we turn to it as a way of carrying on our living.

And in the end, when all is said, humanity is but a microcosm; and we merely perceive little sets of relationships that we call the universe. In this little universe of ours we are turning always toward some manifestation of our life in the person of some figure in it, some fellow vehicle and exemplar of living. The function of acting is to express in terms of a human body some vibrant region of this life of ours; to set before our eyes some epitome of man's vitality; to add to the character and event some element of abstraction that goes beyond and above them, something of that pure and separable element that arises from every artistic expression. This is the object of all art, to create in reality abstraction and in abstraction reality; to complete, in sum, our living for us. It is this that gives to art something of the quality of a dream, the fear for its possibility, the urgency of its desire. And it is this in art that makes life follow it.

NOTES ON ACTING

WHEN you hear a man like Mr. George Copeland play Bach and afterward a Spanish habanera, you get the sense of something fundamentally musical, something that begins with the first phrase and goes on unbroken to the last note of the composition. There is no rapidity and no pause that does not exist in relationship to what is before and after it. The whole of it is one rythm, one magnificent and infectuous continuity. Such playing of such music is like a fine piece of architecture in which the entire unity of all the parts appears and every part takes its life from the whole. The whole progression moves steadily, it is varied but unbroken.

The secret of gesture in acting lies in the fact that there is no movement and no part of any movement that means anything in itself, but only as it ensues from what comes before and proceeds into what comes after. If an actress puts her hand on a man's shoulder the mere moment of the hand's presence has no life in it and no effect. The gesture must begin in the shoulder. Proceeding from the whole body, and even from the whole state of mind, perhaps, it arrives, slow or fast, finally at its objective.

Chaliapin, when the ghost comes to Boris and he drops to his knees on the floor, has in reality only three or four patterns of movement; but these are so related to his entire body and so continuous among themselves that they are able to convey the immense meaning behind them. No little of the secure effect of Charlie Chaplin's pieces of business is due to the fact that, from start to finish, a scene of his possesses an unbroken flow, like music. If an actor raises his hands in supplication toward the sky, the sense of elevation and entreaty will come not only from the gesture's flowing upward to its seeming resting-place, but also from the presence that you sense in the resting hands of their going down again. Duse's bow before the curtain was expressive because it seemed not a mere bending at the hips, but rather to include everything from the feet on which she stood to the thought in her mind and the gentleness of her lowered eyelids. The purity of a gesture consists in the unmarred flow of it through the changes that are related to itself; and its purity of line is lost when these relationships are broken or confused. The average actor makes bad gestures because he can neither think nor move except in patches and unrelated instances.

Art is a process of expressing one part of life in terms of another. An architect expresses the life of his dreams and ideas in terms of his life with visual solid forms. A singer may pour into sound his erotic experience. For this reason it is true that art is not art at all except in so far as it is alive. The characteristic of the living is that it never is at rest but is a perpetual rhythm of change. A moment approaches its most complete establishment, it arrives, but even as it arrives it is breaking down into what comes after. Save for this rhythm toward and from itself, it would be dead; it is alive only in this relative life. The same holds true of all movement on the stage; all of it derives from an unbroken rhythm of the actor's thought, and is alive only within a rhythm of the body that from the actor's entrance to his exit is continuous.

SPEED

No end of the difficulties in the New York serious theatre would be avoided or halved, at least, if the producers insisted more on speed in speaking, and if the actors trained for it. Speed in enunciation and delivery of lines. In

such a play as Regnard's *Le Légataire Universel*
at the Comédie Française, or *Le Cid* or a
modern piece like *Les Marionettes,* the actors
take speeches in something like a third of the
time that a speech of the same length would
require on our stage. This, of course, is due in
part to the language, since the lack of a strong
tonic accent in French and the frequent liaisons
permit a much greater rapidity of utterance.
But it comes partly also from the training and
care that these French actors exercise to ac-
quire mere speed. The tirades, then, for the
French, those long discourses so much objected
to by their English critics, become another
thing, and say more and take no longer than
many of the speeches in our theatre.

Of all this *Back to Methuselah* was a good instance. In those scenes—to take a less tiresome
example of Shaw's garrulity in this play—where
the Brothers Barnabas explain their doctrine,
much would be gained if the actors sat still,
took each other's speeches up immediately,
with distinct and precise enunciation, and
heightened the speed at which the lines are
given. This would be artificial, yes, but that
has no point, for the scenes in themselves are
patently dialogue statements of ideas. Potter-
ing about, changing positions, climbing on
furniture, looking out of windows and the like,
trying to make these scenes seem real, can

accomplish only a childish rubbish of illusion. These scenes are a dramatist's convention from the start, and to admit them frankly as such only keeps the art of them intact. For this speed, of course, there would have to be concentration on the precise accent of word and on the sense accent; and there would have to be trained lips, tongue, and breathing. There would have to be vivacity of tone, concentration on the values of emphasis and idea, and smart accuracy of phrase. But what else is an artist on the stage for?

TEMPO

If you listen in the New York theatre you will very commonly hear actor after actor take the tempo of his speech from the speech that has just been spoken. And so it happens sometimes that for a whole scene the tempo in all the speeches has about the same measure. I doubt if the average producer ever thinks one way or the other about the subject.

But the vitality behind dramatic art makes it necessarily true that every part has in itself its general tempo, its time-pattern; and the same is true of every single speech. What is true of visual design is true for the ear also: that every section of a play is a time-centre in itself, to which surrounding parts are related;

all these centres in their turn are related to larger centres, and so on.

A study of tempo by our actors would help mend two of the worst faults on our stage, monotony and lack of speed. And the achievement of more variety and speed would help to clear away the idly imitative, the realistic clutter now so much in the way of the art of the theatre. And finally a study of tempo leads to better diction, to more flexible characterization, and to a sharper impress of the dramatic pattern involved.

OBVIOUS AND INEVITABLE

Without meaning to in the least, I startled a company of art-lovers by saying that a certain actress-singer was nearly always obvious. She had few tricks, I said, that would not be obvious to the merest nursery-maid in the gallery and would not be expected and exploited by this maid.

To this the host replied that these things were obvious, yes, but all great art was obvious. Obvious and simple, he said.

And just there we touch on one of the main points in the art of the theatre. A great moment in this art is not obvious. In the end it may be so, after the moment is accomplished,

but not till then. What such a moment is, is
not obvious, it is inevitable.

Obvious means that the thing stands out as
what we expected, as what would more or less
naturally ensue. In this obviousness there is
a sense of completeness not because the moment and its implications are exhausted but
because it seems wound up, finished up, or
amazingly exploded; it seems to say to us,
There You Have It. Nazimova in one of her
pieces of business in *Hedda Gabler* is obvious.
It is when Hedda is left alone there in the room
while the men go out to seek Eilert. Nazimova in this scene wears a black gown, an
enveloping sort of robe it is. She goes over to
the door, closed against her exit and leading
to the world outside, and beats her hands des-
perately against it. Then she turns and falls
back against the door, her arms extended in a
cross, and at this point a great splash of crimson flames out where her robe falls open and
shows its lining. You wince at the obviousness of it. Mary Garden has fine moments
and some fine devices, but much of her business sticks out as mere business, focussed and
held by her personal magnetism; and the sense
of inventiveness protrudes rather shamelessly.
The dullest person in the house can see that it
must be effective. And the common stage, of

course, abounds—and unfailingly—with a less inventive form of the obvious, things done that we all entirely expect, that we were born into, that are imitated or plagiarized or traditional.

Inevitable means quite another thing, something that may proceed from the same source as these more obvious devices but exceeds them. Inevitable means that it has something to it that we expected and yet did not expect. It means something that seems unescapable after it is done; and it bears so on the point to be revealed in the moment that only expert eyes can see it as business, the rest of the audience take it as something necessarily there, which is exactly what they should do. When the inevitable is achieved, the moment and its implications are not exhausted at all. And they seem complete not only because they appear to belong absolutely to the occasion but also because they allow for infinite radiation, for infinite possibilities of truth and revelation. A thing in acting seems inevitable because it surprises and satisfies us at once; and because it creates a something there which was not there before. The obvious is like the writing in a copy-book or like an adding-machine; it is all there, or it may startle and delight with its striking inventiveness, but so it ends. The inevitable is like the sun on the wall; it is sim-

ple, complete too, but infinitely subtle, full of
nuance, inexhaustible. Sarah Bernhardt was
often obvious, if any one ever was; but very
often the obvious with her was lifted out of
that plane by style, great recreative style; and
real style, involving as it does the mystery of
personality, can never be obvious.

And great art is simple only through the
fact that it discovers the inevitable something
that will give it unity.

MINOR EXHIBITIONISTS

Among our actors nowadays there is many a
one who, if I should say "Remember to hold
your upper lip that way when you say the word
bitter," would turn on me with contempt or
rage, meaning that I should know better than
to say that sort of thing to an actor; it makes
him self-conscious. And if I say to a certain
young actress that she is to take the first three
words in her speech staccato and raise her chin
as she delivers them, she will complain that she
cannot feel natural doing it that way. And if
I urge another to find one particular gesture
for a certain passage and, having got it, to do
nothing else every night but that gesture, memorizing its exact line, I shall be rebuked as
trying to make acting artificial.

I might reply to these actors that I am not

so much concerned with their being natural as I am with their being interesting; I might say that an actor's business in his art is to learn to use his self-consciousness as he uses any other part of himself; I might say many other things; and it would come to little. What is in these people's heads is the notion that acting must be themselves, and that they must feel the thing they are trying to do, and then act it according to their feelings. They are taking an ingenuous view of art, a middle-class dislike for the admission of artifice and arrangement. They dislike to think that the mind arranges and designs the final expression of the moment of acting; according to them this must arise straight from the actor's feelings at the time.

But feeling the scene is something that no actor can forever depend on; he may upon occasions feel the scene more or less, feel it as before or differently, or not at all. And even if he could be sure of the right excitement within himself, he must remember that the art of acting does not consist only of what is felt, much of it lies in the external means by which feeling is conveyed. The health of acting—as of any other art or of life—is strictly related to the inner experience's arriving at some outer form, without which it never comes wholly into being. And so it is essential that each of these felt moments on the actor's part must find its visual image or embodiment. In this respect a great art in acting would share the character of nature itself; in which the form evinced—the rose, the tiger, the tree—is inseparable from the idea or soul within it; the actor's gesture would image the life within him and the life in him inform the gesture.

Obviously, however, in the acting of a dramatic moment, there are, among the various reactions that the actors may feel, some that are more enduring and significant than others. They go farther, mean more, have more content; and the definite and conscious effort to remember them and to conjure them up again may be of advantage. Meanwhile the fact remains that the process of art is one of alternate inspiration and memory. As the artist works and as he returns again and again to the work, he discovers in himself something that seems suddenly to forward the conception and revelation that his art undertakes. This happy something, often not consciously expected or prepared for, he will recognize, and will strive to remember in order that he may revive it. And so, with one discovery and invention after another, and the memorizing and repeating of them, he may bring into his final expression of the moment such radiant elements as may best create it into a form of art. Among these radiant elements there will be some that are gestures, visible bodies of the ideas working in him, and these, too, he will memorize and repeat.

The ideal for the actor would of course, be that he should be able after due work and inspiration to arrive at some emotion or idea that discovers the profoundest quality in the dramatic moment, the deepest inclusion of life in it; and that every time he acts the moment he should, out of his great genius, recover perfectly and with luminous precision this experience; and that this truth should every time achieve exactly the gesture most capable of embodying and conveying it.

This would be the ideal for the actor certainly, and to be kept always in mind.

But all things in life and art, as we know too well, are subject to imperfection. And the fact remains, more or less apart from all this, that for an emotion we may discover a gesture, a visual movement or line, that can take on a life of its own and can go on conveying successfully an idea to us regardless of what the actor himself may come to feel at the time he is making it. That gesture, then, will be the one that he must use. The most desirable end would be, of course, that the actor fill up the gesture whenever he uses it with the original emotion from which it derived. But often, if one or the other, either the new feeling or the arranged gesture, must be sacrificed, it is better to lose the feeling and keep the gesture.

To deny this and to insist, as so many actors do, and some schools of acting also, on some direct and ingenuous relation always of what they do on the stage to what they feel in themselves at the time, is only to evince a foolish individualism and personal insistence; and to suffer from a kind of exhibitionism by which you want to show yourself willy-nilly; and to make your art the immediate exhibition of whatever you are at the moment, as if it were yourself and not the moment that is the thing to be shown.

This insistence is not only vulgar and insignificant; it shows an ignorance of the essential character of form and of the nature of all art and all creation, which is constantly releasing forms that possess their own separable and independent life and meaning.

And finally, there is something uncultured and barbarous in this whole attitude. The physical body achieves forms and forces that can bridge it over the times when it is not functioning at its best; a man achieves ideas and moral conceptions that carry him over the inequalities and saggings of his mental and moral existence; men in societies achieve laws and systems that sustain the life of the group when conditions falter; and so with the achievements of sustaining forms in an art. Culture, as distinguished

from mere instinct and improvisation, begins
with the knowledge of this fact.

There was a moment in *Œdipus Rex* as
Mounet-Sully played it when Œdipus is reduced
to the last despair; everything has been taken
from him, his honor, his children, his mother
and wife, his kingdom and friends. And when
he came to this point Mounet-Sully descended
the palace steps and lay down flat on the ground.
At every performance and on the same word he
did that. In that gesture the whole moment was
revealed; his body went back again to the bosom
of the earth from which it came; he was a part
of the doom and motherhood of nature; in him
human life returned to its first elements. Once
achieved, that gesture almost departed from any
mood that the actor himself might have at any
performance of the scene. It had become more
important than any mood that he might have.
In it Mounet-Sully had discovered a something
that goes on even now in my mind as the most
essential idea and tragic content of that scene.
He had found what became the body of the idea,
something as inevitable and complete as music.

WONDER IN ACTING

The prosaic or unimportant actor, if he works
seriously, can satisfy his audience by getting
what they expect. In a scene, a line, an emo-

tional reaction, he produces an effect that can be seen at once to be what was due; it is sensible and reasonable. And what this actor does at these satisfactory and gratifying moments is not wrong; it violates no probability but takes its place in the logical sequence of the emotion, the idea, the situation. It can be workmanlike, ample, and commendable. Such an actor will win nods of approval from all over the house. He is a good, working journeyman.

The important actor is not like this. What he does is true and satisfying, also, unless it be at times too much of a strain for people incapable of response or understanding or sympathetic energy. What this actor does also fits the sequence of the emotion, the idea, the situation. But it is never wholly expected. There is about all talent—which is the thing that makes a piece of art living instead of dead—about all manifestations of talent, a continual slight surprise. When a real talent on the stage reads a line or presents an emotion, we recognize the truth of it. It is reasonable to the deepest content of the moment. It satisfies our need for the suitable, the fitting; but it also delights us by something in the actor's tone, his emotional reaction, his idea, that we had no particular reason to expect; something that is a little different and additional; something, indeed, that has upon it the mystery of what is alive.

In the world of nature there is nothing—a rose, a tiger, a tree—of which we can say that we quite know what it is before it comes into actual existence. By just this identity with and this inseparability from its own creation and birth, and by just the presence in it of something that arrives only with its arrival, a living thing in nature differs from a dead thing that we might manufacture. The actor must strive always to discover for the rendering of a moment of his art, for a tone, a gesture, a piece of stage business, an element of something that could not have been foreseen or expected, though it is immediately recognized as expressive and revealing; something that perhaps surprises even himself, as coming from parts of himself or sources of life which are imperfectly known by him; something that comes into being only when the moment comes into being that it reveals and is. Only through this can he give us what is not alone an explanation of the dramatic moment but also the creation of it.

And so in the art of acting it is the revelation of some ultimate reasonableness rather than mere expected logic, of something luminous as well as convincing, that distinguishes talent from intent. There is always about a moment of fine acting a kind of fringe of wonder.

THE VOICE IN THE THEATRE

IF THE psychology of our day has stressed anything it is the fact that the life of the mind rests on historically ancient processes, on the constituted matter of the universe. That is to say we are grown out of and into nature; we are a part of its texture, of its tissue even; and what we call ourselves is only the little conscious point at which we connect with the whole, and through which we enter on a conception of the whole. The life of the mind has the same relation to nature as the fragrance of a flower has to the earth; our consciousness is the light fragrance of a flower, but this fragrance is the odor of reality. It is only through all this accumulated history that is in us, the remembering organisms, the unforgetting cells and growths, that we share in the life of the world. And only through the exploitation and use of this sharing can we express for the rest of the whole the living part of it that we are.

It follows, then, that art depends first of all on the life of the body, that body which is at the same time the ancient storehouse of the forms and pulses and directions of a whole; and is yet its feeling organ, its every moment's intimate perceiving. In the art of the theatre, then, to throw away such an avenue as is the sense of sound is shortsighted and suicidal. It is a way of limiting the expression of life, of forgetting the necessary earth, of telling lies. And in our theatre it is a fact that sound is almost a forgotten thing. The voice is used in our theatre almost entirely as an articulate medium. But a part of every truth is its inarticulateness; all the half-conscious elements, delicate implications, the radiant and shadowy emanations that make up every human truth, and that words can never express. And sound itself has significance. The articulate meaning of the word *pain* is a symbolistic accident; the sound of it goes vaguely but farther in. Regardless of word concepts the mere voice is another medium to express the ancient and imminent life that lives itself in us.

Every one knows the part a dramatist's sound takes in his complete effect. Shakespeare obviously is always recognized first of all by the ear. Very much of Galsworthy's failure to convince me, I think, lies in the pedestrian and easy drought of his music. And I believe that one of the obstacles of Ibsen's progress with us, something that makes his work seem dry and dutiful and Euclidian, is the sterile sound of the acting translations: a humble ear would take Mrs. Alving for Madame President calling the ladies to

order, and stating her case for their consideration. Every dramatist has his own voice and
every language has its voice. But it must be re-
membered that the voice is inextricably tied up
with its language. We complain of the Italian
singer's voice as "white"; but Italian is a "white"
language. We complain of the German tone as
"dark"; but German, and English too, are "dark"
languages. Mimi Aguglia's voice, amazing in
Italian, animal, pathetic, inexhaustible, becomes
light, uninteresting, when she speaks English.
Miss Doris Keane is the only actor I have ever
seen who could reproduce in English the Italian
tone exactly, not to mention the enchanting persuasion and fascination she puts into it.

The voice of a country's theatre, like the English or French or Italian, gets to be as definite
perhaps as an actor's. There is the American
stage voice with its tone driven through the
nose, its inflexible upper lip, its bad placement
in the throat, and its frequent monotony. There
is the voice the English practice, with its dry,
balanced quality, suited so well to their social
comedy but lacking in range and fluency, too
full of aspirated breath, and without much met-
tle or resonance in the head; the French voice
with its trained production, and its adequacy for
dramatic uses; the moving Russian voice; the
Italian voice, the best of all, a free tone, a tragic
timbre, a wide range and abundance of power.

Style in the use of voice implies in one sense a personal distinction. But in general it means a use of the voice that finds the same essential quality that the matter to be said possesses. Style in an actor's or a theatre's voice would mean a constant variation of the timbre, the delivery and enunciation to suit the kind of play it carries or the mood. In a comedy of manners like *The School for Scandal*, for example, the voice would be clear, finished, the lips expert, the tongue striking well on the teeth; the tone would go up and down but always be sure of its place in the throat, be crisp, shining, in hand, like the satin and gold of the furniture and costumes, the rapier at the wrist, the lace over it, the worldliness, and the wit. In Chekhov it would have the last naturalness, every closeness to feeling and impulse that the moment reveals. In Shakespeare a range of elaborate music, suited to the style, a clearness, with a warmth of poetic emotion. In D'Annunzio's drama the voice would have to be rich and sensuous, metallic, shading infinitely, the voice of a degenerate god. And so on through the styles and moods of all drama.

It is, of course, a platitude in æsthetics to say that music is the most ideal of the arts. Music can be the thing itself where words can only be the concept of it or painting one selected phenomenon. In the light of this you may say that an actor's voice is his most important medium.

You may say that the tone an actor uses can move us more than any other thing about him. The word he speaks gives the concept, the gesture he makes exhibits a single phenomenon; but the voice may be anger itself or longing, and may go straight, as music does, to the same emotion in us. So that there is something strange and ironical in the realization of how much more our theatres—and our education for that matter —have cultivated the eye rather than the ear. We have all sorts of instructions about stage production, about light and its uses and diversities, about the effect of colors and their combinations. In Gordon Craig's design for *Electra* we have the idea of that door, high and fateful and unrevealing, the domination of visual proportion over our sense. In the best settings we have sometimes had light and color and line made as ideal almost and as abstract as music. But, after all, that concerns the realm of the visual, it is eye-learning.

And so we may well recall what education the Greeks thought wise for the uses of their sons. Philosophy, rhetoric, oratory and recitation, and music, were the main branches of their endeavor. Sculpture and painting and architecture, those arts whose life is in the eye, they learned to know by seeing them and by the images arising from the perfecting of their bodies in the daily palestra. But often enough the philosophy that they learned, the history and poetry and logic, came through discourses and argument and reading aloud, and much of what they knew well they may never have seen in writing; they had received it in sound-images instead of visual. In Athens the ear of a man of culture was trained to hear the value of syllables and rhythm and cadence in speech, the modes of music and the quality of the voice in reading and singing.

In the Theatre of Dionysos the lighting was that of the sun; the scene was but slightly varied either through shifts or through light. The gestures were simple and restrained, as we may infer from the spirit and the style of the plays, and may be sure of from the difficulties that the costume, the onkos, the padding, and the high-soled cothurnus would have put in the way of animated motions. The expression of the mask remained unchanged, but it was made so as to serve as a resonator for the actor's voice. So that the larger part of the effect in the Greek theatre was due to the voices, trained as we train for the opera and exerted for a trained public taste. However beautiful the lines of those garments may have been, their grave and exquisite rhythms and their subtlety of color in the bright air, the blowing on them of the wind from the Bay of Salamis, it was the voices of the actors that achieved much of that effect of tragic beauty. The words of the dramatist were conveyed through the voice, animated by the beauty and variety of its music; and sometimes heightened further still by the music of pipes and strings that followed the voice, dilating further the poetic meaning, making it yet more poignant and unerring.

"*Cynthius aurem vellit, et admonuit,*" Virgil wrote, when the god of poetry came to him; and Milton, translating, "Phœbus replied, and touched my trembling ears."

To all that antique world the ear was the seat of memory. And memory is half our life, and more than half of all beauty.

TALENT

I REMEMBER several years ago seeing Miss Doris Keane as the prima donna in Edward Sheldon's *Romance*. I remember how startled I was. There was a voice that went straight to its objective, hit the ear like a gesture. The sudden, startling vivacity of tone leapt out in a speech now and then like a red bird out of the shadows; the laugh cut like a bright whip across the moment. There was a fine plastic gift, a living use of the hands; the wrists were eloquent in their lines. There was a beautiful floating movement across the stage when the actress walked, an urgent and compelling pantomime. And finally, there was over everything done a sense of a certain droll pungency of intelligence. And all these qualities seemed to be somehow the actress' body; her very presence seemed to be the truth of them.

For talent is ultimately a thing of the body. It goes back to the body as music does to the ear-drum and the nerves of hearing; it gives an important continuity to the person, and makes it not only true but necessary that the greatest actors always in a sense act themselves. But what talent may be, with all its separability, vividness, vitality, and magnetism, you cannot say exactly. Talent in an actor has a mysterious difference from mere capacity for hard work, though work perfects it by sifting out its special and right mode of expression, and so frees it to be its essential self. It differs from intention, however earnest; for talent is an organic thing—to take a term from science—as distinguished from inorganic; it is a part of the structure, the organism, the living tissue of the person who possesses it rather than something to be taken on, desired, and labored at. And talent is an immediate thing. To those who have an eye for it, talent is discernible at once when it comes on the stage; it establishes a kind of luminosity of the presence, a radiance of the body seen to be living out the moment there. When an actor with talent is on the stage with actors who have none, he seems to stand apart from them, to flow toward them and from them, to be a living thing separate from the rest, who appear to be surroundings in which creation has not yet happened. It is the quality of this difference that indicates the reason why talent is inexpressible. Only through its own manifestation can talent, like all things that are a part of nature, convey itself completely to us.

THE TRAGIC GOOSE-STEP

I REMEMBER once, on an autumn afternoon, seeing a matinée of poetic plays, or rather scenes from them, given by a group of young actors at a certain theatre. The plays were Elizabethan, scenes from Marlowe, Beaumont and Fletcher, and the somewhat later Otway. There was a separate director for each dramatist represented.

I arrived late, ten minutes or so. And as my eye lighted on the scene I saw that a dialogue had just closed; the lady stood in the middle of the stage and the gentleman was in the act of departing, moving toward a door in the wings. My attention was at once caught by his unusual movement. His hips seemed at each step to congeal themselves, to become rigid, and from this rigid pivotage the leg shot out toward the floor, a straight, inflexible line. And as the heel of each foot struck the floor, the impact registered in the hip above it and the whole body made a solemn vibration of resistance to the trodden earth beneath. The nostrils, too, grew firmer.

I watched the various scenes. The young ladies in them seemed to have little idea at all of what was to be done. You got the general impression that if one wears a snood like a lady of Marlowe's time, one must have a rosebud mouth and a virginal, versified cast of countenance. The artistic creed set forth most strongly seemed to be a demonstration of the fact that the human body looks well enough without stays after all, and that if one stands a little sway-backed in a long white robe with a slanting girdle or rope of pearls around one's waist and dropping between one's knees, one can indicate a creditable enough figure of a woman. As for the verse, that was spoken smoothly, ravingly, chantingly, stertorously, or in a sublime calm above all mere meaning or sense, in whatever way fortune willed. But if the reading varied, the step was everywhere, the getting across the stage was always the same, and no artist failed to register its measured delays and stalking rhythm. To that extent at least the entire afternoon was uniform.

At last it was clear to me what this stride was about; this tragic goose-step, so inexplicable otherwise, meant that we were acting poetry. It was the gait of immortality, the ritual of bardolatry. And then I realized how well it might serve as a symbol for most of the trouble that blocks the way of our poetic drama.

In our theatre the minute we recognize that a thing is poetry we make something separate of it. We give the poetic a sort of worship; which means, as Bernard Shaw said once of heroes, that everybody bows down to it and nobody does its will. To do the will of poetry is to take it naturally.

But we Anglo-Saxons are a great race for setting things apart, for separating them from our plain and usual tracks. Even religion we tend to separate from us. The spirit of it may be in our daily living, but the expression, the celebration of it, and especially its more formal celebration, we set off to itself. We carry no chickens, ducks, or vegetables into church with us.

Whereas in Italy or in Spain people come into the church as they might cross a street. There is no change in the natural habitude of that more serious region. They kneel, if they are simple folk, with their baskets at their sides, and watch the heart-shaped candle flames on the altar ahead of them, the incense rising in the dusk, the motions of the priest, the vestments, the music, the words repeated over and over. And they know that this is only another department of life, in no way different from the rest, a part of our natures needing expression. They know that here these motions and the mood of this ceremony become formal and graver only because they may thus become natural to the thing expressed; that the remoteness of the expression is there only because in this more ultimate region of the day's living there is remoteness and the simplification of our thought and spirit.

And so in poetry. In our theatre, acting poetic plays is a kind of going to church, as we use the word, with all the awe, particularity, tedium, and unfrequentedness implied. The very legs of those actors I saw were stiffened with their poetic specialty, this apartness of verse; and with it their throats were routed. But in Spain the audience scarcely knows when the play is prose and when it is verse, or when, as happens there so often, the same play passes back and forth from one to the other. Every year around Hallowe'en in Madrid, Zorilla's *Don Juan Tenorio* is given for five nights in all the principal theatres. And there is no actor in it but goes from prose to verse and back again without batting an eyelash and with the utmost naturalness. And in Italy the same audience and the same actors experience the gorgeous poetry of D'Annunzio or the beautiful, warm, marble quality of Morselli, and the realism of Giacosa and Marco Praga without any specializing whatever. And so with them the realm of poetry is ventilated, is healthy and natural.

In our theatre the health and the possibility of creating and of acting poetic drama lies in our understanding one fact: that there is no difference in kind between what we call poetic and what we call prose. No difference in kind. We may have arrangements obviously, genres if you like, in verse or in prose. But on the whole they are related to each other, the poetic and the prosaic, exactly as the moments of life are related to each other. In life, for instance, we have particular moments of deep feeling, say, or suspense. We do not separate these, hold them compartmentally off to themselves. What happens is a gradual heightening, an intensification of our beings. The pulse concentrates its stroke, it is quicker or it seems almost suspended; but its existence is deepened and made more compulsive. The body increases its life, it moves toward more complete unity. The mind is charged with a vaster region in which it dilates and seems to breathe a wider air. The whole of us, mind, body, spirit, is driven toward a simplification, a oneness. We draw more easily and luminously a radiance from ourselves and from the life of the world that we have shared. And though all this may happen in a graver or a lighter mood, the point remains the same. The poetic in our existence differs in no way generically from prose, exactly as the moments of a life do not differ in kind but only in completeness from one another. And that is what the poetic is in the art of the theatre. The rhythm, the word, the incident do not essentially change. They are only driven down into their inmost substances. By a heightening in vitality they are simplified;

and through that, at the same moment they are made more subtle. They become more accurate, which is to say truer to the experience expressed.

For an actor or a producer when these plays of the poetic sort are presented, what ought to happen does not necessarily mean any change in method as compared to the prose play. Even in Racine, to take an extreme case, the method changes only in the sense that it fits itself to an accepted and confessed conventionalization of idea and form. And in the poetic drama as we have it in English—in most of it at least—there need be no change whatever. All that need happen is what happens in our lives. Where the intensity and accuracy of effect approaches a larger and simpler order or a more passionate ornament in beauty and imagined grace, there the gesture, the delivery, the expression follow. Good verse follows its content exactly. It is in form precisely true to its sense. To read it, then, requires no ramping about like he-muses marching to Parnassus, no startled reverence, but only an increased exactitude.

The only reverence, then, that is worth while in art is not one that jerks the legs about, blows up the lungs and gets the soul on a high horse. It is a reverence that, once under way, is scarcely conscious of itself save for the quiet amplitude or the beautiful ease or absorbing intensity or passion or elevation or clarity or spacious precision that has come into the moment.

BEAUTY AND THE BEAST

WHEN the Theatre Guild took down Andreyev's book from the library shelf and put it on the stage, it presented one of the most charming plays of the season. Under the picturesque title of *He Who Gets Slapped* there unfolds for us a story of a wise man who, having found his wife and his trusted friend false to him and that the world did not understand him, comes at last and joins Papa Briquet's circus. There he finds the beautiful maiden, Consuelo, who loves the handsome bareback rider, Bezano. But her supposed father, Count Mancini, the decayed aristocrat, a droll figure with his odd clothes and his pompous airs, wishes Consuelo to wed the baron, a fat, horrid man but blessed with much gold. The lion-tamer, Zinida, loves Bezano also, and has strange ideas about her red lion's loving her. He—which is the name the newcomer assumes when he buries his life and its secrets in the ranks of the circus—has the droll wish to be slapped; and it turns out that the audience thinks this very funny indeed. He falls in love with Consuelo, who is a simple girl quite unable to understand the great love of the poor clown or his wise, quaint sayings. Finally the baron, since he cannot have Consuelo any other way, proposes marriage. Her father, Count Mancini, accepts with alacrity. On her farewell day in the ring the baron has Consuleo's whole path carpeted with red roses. All the circus people are invited to drink champagne during one of the intermissions, the bride's health and happiness, at the rich baron's expense. But Consuelo, though too innocent to know what fate really confronts her with the loathsome baron, is hysterical when he merely touches her. He, the clown, seeing all this, gives her a drink of poison and takes the same for himself. And so he saves her from the horror of this beast that was to possess her, and he dies with her, happy that he can meet her in worlds to come and lay his love forever at her little feet.

For such a story as this the acting at the Garrick is excellent, exactly keyed; though Mr. Calvert's rôle and his art happen to be such as might fit into quite another play also. And Mr. Simonson's setting for all this is charming, the picturesque properties of the scene especially; though the use of different levels and the fine line of arches at the back might imply a graver and bigger idea than its play shows. Miss Gilmore is not an actress yet, for her technic is still in the schoolgirl stage, but she has an appealing quality and a genuine feeling for the tragic little life that she portrays. He—Mr. Bennett—is perhaps a little mild, but lovable and quaint and pathetic. Miss Westley as Zinida smokes her cigarettes, and swaggers about quite as a true lion tamer in such a romance would do. And Mr. Frank Reicher, in spite of his forcing all the time and registering too much and too often in a tiresome movie manner, is every inch the Italian count of the stage, with his walk, his ridiculous voice, his lofty ways. Mr. Rutherford's Bezano smacks his lips down too much over his words when he talks; but he is a fine, strong young fellow, a hundred-per-cent man, just such a lover as Consuelo would choose. Except for a phrase now and then that threatens to complicate the true meaning of the story, and except for a little foreign something which even the simplest person in the audience scents as being mysterious and Russian, the play sails smoothly; and if one tends to sag at any time into depths of perplexity, a single look at Mr. Reicher mincing and jerking about so drolly or at Mr. Bennett's soft mass, will serve to reassure one of the lovable and engaging atmosphere of the piece. It is all as quaint and sad and adorable as an old fairy story; the hints and mysteries and provocative sayings that are left here and there only add a certain originality and modernity. This play is delightful and well worth doing for itself, I think, and one of the best things in town. It is

wistful and appealing all through, and, what's
more, it is always consistent.

But there can be no harm surely in speaking
also of the play that Andreyev wrote and that
is known in Russia; or in saying that the Guild
production is wrong, though consistently wrong,
throughout, and that it departs from the real
play to an extent which, if it only went in the
reverse direction, would make it an important
original creation.

He Who Gets Slapped is the story of a man,
a philosopher, who leaves the world which has
never understood him and which has cheapened
all his finest thoughts—a motive that has a simpler parallel in his wife's desertion of him for
his inferior imitation—and comes to join a circus. Here under the clown's ridiculous garb he
will say his great thoughts, tell the crowd what
wise and beautiful ideas arise in him, and get
himself slapped and laughed at for a fool; when
all the while the mockery and the jest are at
their expense. In the company there is Consuelo, not a mere young girl, but the figure of
all beauty, white and rose and gold, ignorant of
the world, untouched. She is the centre of all the
love motives in this play that turns on love in
all its kinds; and is herself the ideal thing, unconscious of itself, desired by all the others. And
there, too, is Bezano, beautiful, cruel, destroying, as life and passion are destroying. He, the

clown, loves Consuelo for herself and because
she is the image of all beauty. And in the end
he kills her to save her from the defilement of
the baron's hands; and he dies with her, following beauty out of the world as he had followed
it all his life, and slapped and jeered and misun-
derstood to the very last by the crowd about
him.

This is Andreyev's play, a tragic fantasy
around the ironical career that truth and distinction meet at the hands of the common mass
of men. *He Who Gets Slapped* is not a great
play. The beginning is superb, especially the
passages where the mysterious stranger states
his reasons for joining the circus and his philosophy of life—difficult and suggestive passages
which seemed to be shortened in the Guild production—but the end of the play spreads out
into a looser hold and—though this indefinable
and insoluble mood may very well enhance a
certain effect of significant chaos—lacks the
sense of fine artistic control. So that it remains a
remarkable second-rate play, but one of the
most remarkable in the modern theatre. *He
Who Gets Slapped* is a bitter, lovely thing, full
of an intellectual passion in which all beauty is
exalted and the drabness and commonness of
men is perpetually mocked. Its poetry is glowing and bitter and cruel at bottom; its pathos
under the picturesque poignancy is profound

and elusive and sinister, and the gaiety and bus-
tle of its action is an irony on the foolish stir of
our living above its hidden depth and beauty,
the life of the soul in the midst of the circus.

All this quality underlies the character of He
himself. But would any one mistake Mr. Bennett
for anything beyond a dear, droll, plump, romantic booby, never very keen, never very complex, never bitter and mordant, though very generous and arch and lovable and pathetic? And
in the Zinida at the Garrick where is the smoul-
dering tragic darkness of the magnificent animal, the command, the tiger burning bright?
Mr. Calvert's art is consummate; Mr. Travers as
Jackson, the clown, is good in the first scene.
But the worst acting of all, if we take the play
from Andreyev and not from the surrounding
version, is that of Mr. Frank Reicher. For the
part of Mancini, Andreyev in his directions is
explicit enough: the count is ragged in places,
macabre, absurd, fallen so low that the only
place for his lording it is among these circus
people. Mancini is used as an ironical underscoring of the central character; for exactly as
the case of He, the thinker, presents a mockery
of the mind and imagination and truth, so Mancini, the nobleman, carries about him a travesty
of fallen aristocracy, and of what happens to
these high aristocratic qualities of pride and
form and style in the individual himself and in

the crowd's opinion of them when they are no longer sustained by money. Mancini is a fantastic satire in black and white against the color of his surroundings. But Mr. Reicher only minces and struts around like the French count in old-fashioned melodrama, and misses entirely the deeper, grave and bizarre and tragic absurdity that life has come to in this man.

In a sense the Guild production is more of a unit than Andreyev's play. Andreyev took something of an old-style clown story, and roughened and weighted the texture with his extravagant comment and fecundity; and this Guild production smooths it back again to the simpler story. Nearly everything in the play fits together now; though it must be said that the resulting harmony is like reducing the wind and the elements of the world to a melody played on a music-box.

In this pleasing fashion the performance was one that I enjoyed, and I am thankful to the Guild for undertaking even one of the many plays that lie in this curiously difficult and modern drama. And then, having enjoyed it, I may remark on so perfect an example of how art—as well as life—tends on its weaker side to evade the sting of reality and truth.

TO CHARLIE CHAPLIN, 1920

DEAR MR. CHAPLIN: You get many letters, doubtless, thanking you for all your comicalities, and there are the critics, of course, taking you as a lively comic, but never, so far as I happen to have seen as yet, concerned with you as an artist. We have now your last picture—which they say completes your contract and leaves you free to do what you like. I hope you will do just that and will go on to a larger field.

This is how it stands. You have created one of the great clowns of all time. This Charlie of yours needs no portrait anywhere; he is foolish, pathetic, irrepressible, flickering, comical, lovable beyond all words; he is light as air; he is a blunderer with a heart not solid but worn like a flower on a child's sleeve; a sexless gallantry; he is a tireless curiosity drawn to things as a monkey to a peep-hole or a moth to a flame; a gentle blithe dreamer and acrobat; a mask; he is a small, grotesque music; a dear laughter carried lightly in everybody's breast; a gay, shy classic; a world figment.

But you have finished your creation. It was perfect long ago. Already it begins to slow down.

It shows a falling off in invention and zest; it shows a kind of boredom in you despite the great art with which you sustain the flow of it, the lightness, the airy intensity. Better still it is than all the clowns in the world put together could do, or comic artists anywhere; but it is yet not quite its own best; it is a little weak judged by itself. You have the achievement of it, however, to rest on, whatever happens, whatever you turn to. And you have your own genius and accomplishments to go forward on. The greatest actor in English you are very easily. You have a technic completely finished for your needs so far; an absolute accuracy of the body and the idea, a perfect identification of gesture and intention. You have the musical quality without which no acting is consummate; it appears in your incomparable fluidity of action and in your beautiful, unbroken continuity of style. You have precision and extraordinary economy. You have invention. And—what is the last test—you have been able to give to all this craft and abundance of technical resource that final genius of vitality that makes it really universal, makes it of the people, who long ago recognized your credit though your craft was hid from them.

But with all this you have done only one thing. Why not go on? There are so many that you could do. There is *Liliom* for example. What could you not do with that part where Mr. Schildkraut made it a rôle that was expert only, always crowded in motif and business and nearly always touched with vulgarity and insistence? You could do *He Who Gets Slapped.* Or with study you could do Peer Gynt, and many other parts. But better than all of these, you could do new things written by you or for you, things in which you would use your full endowment, comic and otherwise. And finally you might do what is of all things the most important so far as moving-pictures go, and that is to develop what is calculated strictly for it and for no other art, and is made up out of its essential quality, which is visual motion and not mere stage drama photographed. In sum, you might really create in terms of the moving-picture as you have already created in terms of character.

But all this will have to be a real change, Mr. Chaplin, or at least a real and definite openness to change and to new embarkations. It cannot be done by writing Charles instead of Charlie on the bill-boards, or altering the make-up of your eyes and mustache or shortening your riotous shoes. Such ventures in change amount to nothing and get nowhere. Go in at your full tilt. Go in for what you yourself like, for what satisfies you completely. And say that if the taste of the public does not like your work the taste of the public will have to change.

I think we can all understand some of the difficulties you have to struggle with when you think of taking such a step. There is first of all the natural desire to hold on to what you have won for yourself, to your enormous following. And always, of course, there are people around you who at the very mention of it will tell you that you will lose your place in the sun; who will try to hold you back, out of ignorance or kind solicitude or avarice or jealousy or general timidity. And there is the dread that you might feel of having your serious efforts laughed at, though you can master that if you choose, and can even use it to great ends, use superbly this tension and confusion of laughter and tears together. And not least in your way there is the peculiar money standard in our theatre, not the love of money exactly but its acceptance as a gauge of success, a measure of an actor's height; and you, naturally, may be human enough to compete with the others on their own grounds, however little they can compete with you on what is really yours. But all this is obvious.

The truth is, you—like many an artist and many men not artists in America just now—are at the cross-roads. You have got to choose. It grows clearer and clearer to us all that we are like children getting what we want, but what we want only in competition with each other, not profoundly, not out of ourselves. As time goes on and our relative values get more and

more defined, we observe that much of the kind
of success we see means only more gasolene,
more food, more Victrola records made by other
people, more motion. It is forced on us that if we
want more life we must look ahead to get it, and
must choose what after all we will go after if we
are not to be lost. We can see at any artists' club
the crowd of such as have taken for their art the
watchword of business success, poor wise ar-
rivals who knew how to play the game, knew
what the public wanted and put it over, as soap
and collars and varnishes are put over with us,
and who are now empty-faced, gregarious, un-
subtle, unoriginal, bored, vivacious, and stale.
The necessity for a choice has grown very clear.
These last few years especially for many an artist
and many another man have been a comment on
that experience that Francis Thompson wrote of,
that divine pursuit, that flight down the nights
and days and arches of the years, and the laby-
rinthine ways of one's own mind, and in the
midst of tears, and under running laughter, from
those strong feet that followed, followed after.
The folly of that flight is one of those spiritual
practicalities we cannot dodge, it is the common
sense of the soul.

And whatever you may think, the cold facts
remain, the truth in plain-song. Your public has
had an instinct. It has liked the right thing, the
best to be had. But the large public is like the

natural world: it uses up for its own ends what it finds and then throws it aside. For a while, then, your great public will like, as it has liked, your best art as it comes along. Then later you will have the humiliation and the disillusionment of seeing them applaud equally or even more loudly—partly as the fruit of long habit—your less good things, applaud the bad more than the good was applauded. And this is the bitter last scene of all for a great artist, who can only sustain it easily by increased vanity and egotism. The public's way—which is nature's—of using and throwing aside is right almost, however cruel; for otherwise we should have in the end a survival of what is worse than dead. And yet there is a degree of devotion and survival that is a good thing. There is a degree of permanence of interest and of ideal relationship to art, among cultured men, that is good for art and its complete unfolding; just as there is a degree— though strictly limited and easily carried to unhealthy excess—of sublimation of the natural body into something of more ideality and a more permanent essence. And this you would find among a more cultured audience, of the judicious, as Hamlet would say, however few they might be at first compared to your old millions. And then, too, there is the hard biological fact not to be blinked, of your going off, the sheer physical decline from perfection. And, whether that descent has already begun or not, it is certain at least that this particular thing that you have done is possible physically only a few years more. The spring will go out of it.

And, in conclusion, dear Mr. Chaplin, the main thing is that you be happy as an artist in your own living. And that one can see from your pictures you are not. You have your dreams, we can see that, a passionate and delicate insurgence within you, a poetry and a music and a poignancy that eats into you. One feels that this man we see there on the screen knows very well that most of the people around him know little about him; knows that he has accepted too much cheap praise already and inferior court. He knows that he, like any creative artist, must always be alone and strange, as the mystery of creation is always alone in the material world; he must always be alone exactly as that little figure of his Charlie always stands out from any scene around him by its wistful lustre and pathetic vividness. And this pathos, but half expressed, is what gives you now a good part of your appeal —for even little boys want to take you in their arms as they do their teddy-bears. It is like the pathos of life itself, which arises from our sense in life of the half-expressed, the passionate and tender and violent pushing against the dumb obstacles of fact and matter. If in your work this pathos goes no farther than it does now, it will in time be lessened and gradually become a gap, a lack, or a mere pitifulness and half defeat. But if you carry what is yourself farther toward its full expression in a more complete art, you will express more life, something more beautiful, comic, tragic, and profoundly characteristic of you. That, of course, is what you want, one sees it behind that mask of yours. And it seems only fair to tell you that there are those among your admirers who want you to have it, and believe that you need not fail except as every artist must fail, by comparison, as Leopardi said, with your own dream.

TO DUSE, 1922

MADAME: We are told here that you are coming and that you are not coming. I saw you many years ago in *La Gioconda,* in *Paolo and Francesca,* in *La Citta Morta* and in *Magda,* before you withdrew from the stage. And now that you have returned to the theatre, you will find us hoping in America that you will come again. We hear that you go on the stage with only the glamour of your intense sincerity, without any puppetry, with a make-up not meant to create any illusion but solely to accentuate, with your gray hair admitting life as it stands in you under the sad laws of time, and showing to all who will read it there the writing on you of your real and ideal living. One knows that you would do just this, and that like a great artist you would admit your medium for what it is and work within it.

Those who have never seen you, madame, have heard how you played. They have heard how you seemed to put into the art of acting a modernity so simple and translucent that it seemed as old as the theatre. They have heard of the oneness of your art, the quiver and directness of your playing. They have heard how single your quality was, though the rôles might vary, as the light is single in which the various world is revealed. They have noticed that people who have understood you wish somehow to protect you, as if one were shy about your exquisiteness. And they have seen your photograph.

The face, madame, that they see there holds them. It has something more moving than the more immediately poetic or outwardly beautiful can be; what this face has is a kind of realism of tragic beauty. It has in it the thing that is most terrible and that we worship in life, that last and exquisite thing in life: a supreme response to it. We look at your face and feel that a sob is there, but withheld through the force of the general and universal poignancy and tragic intelligence behind it. Madame, whenever I read Dante, the picture of you keeps coming before my eyes.

The reader of our English poetry coming fresh on Dante for the first time, turns his hungry and astonished eyes on a passage like that of the two lovers who went together and seemed so light on the wind; and reads

"Amor condusse noi ad una morte,"

and then Francesca's words when they read how the beloved smile was kissed by such a lover, and this one who never should be divided from her kissed her mouth all trembling,

"Quando legemmo il disiato riso
  esser baciato da cotanto amante,
  questi, chi mai da me non sia diviso,
  la bocca mi bació tutto tremante":

And a long way farther on in the book he comes
on those lines about human desires and the end
of day, the hour when longing returns to sailors
and penetrates the heart, *intenerisce il core,* the
day that they have said good-by to their sweet
friends; and the new wanderer, *lo novo peregrin,*
is pierced with love if he hears far-off bells that
seem to weep the dying day. And the reader is
amazed. Never before has he read anything in
poetry so close, so free, so tender and direct and
pitiful and exact.

Madame, that poetry has the permeation, the
tender exactitude, that is your art. And like that
poetry it might have happened yesterday, it
might not happen until to-morrow, the thing
I remember as your acting.

Madame, we need you in America to remind
us that for every man there is only his kind of
truth to make in the end any sense for him. The
only purpose for him is that which, to use
Dante's phrase, will give him wax to light him
to his summit. The rest is competition, tricks,
unrest, and satiety without exercise. You force
into everything the soul of its reality; and so
expose its truth or its incapacity and falseness.
Whatever kind of part you take, romantic, rol-

licking comic, poetic, or highly naturalistic, you give the same truth to it by living out and bringing to completion its characteristic quality. Your art is your own perpetual dilation of reality. You have no false purposes, you never conclude, you never solve, you only create and reveal. Most of all, madame, our young actors need you.

These young actors, plenty of them, have talent, have dreams. But they are confused. They see promiscuous advertising and press comment that seems to assure them that they may follow as great artists actors who have nothing to go on but personality, insolence, ignorance, or superficial charm or good luck. These young actors have few good models of anything except success. They hear on all sides that acting copies nature, that their business is to reproduce what they see in life. And so they try, the better of them, to copy nature before they have eyes to see it with. They are given parts that seem by mere resemblance and the accident of individual characteristics to fit them, and they are kept in these parts. They are told practical points and try to carry those points out in order to carry themselves over the footlights and beyond to the electric signs over the doors. These young actors want to get on, that is only human. But they need to learn to express what they themselves have to express; they need to lean on life, not on expedients. They need to see that in you always there is something that the great artists must always have, something that baffles, something withheld. What we get in you, madame, is only the echo of all you are. And this will teach them the emptiness of the poor little show of themselves that they make. You are the artist and the performance is yours; but behind all that, as the world of nature is behind a flower, is you. You are an actor but first you are yourself.

Madame, you can teach these young actors what realism is. They are confused. Half a century of prose and thin science and problems have taught them that realism is the matter-of-fact, the provable and visible and immediately logical. They think that realism is brutality, is the journalistic, the photographic or the drab. In modern drama they have learned a self-conscious social sense; they become not so much artists as they do judges. Those who cannot create have been obliged to solve.

Madame, you know what realism is. To you, from the very start, the theatre, as Huysmans said of schools in literature, is neither realistic nor poetic; it is only good or bad, true or false. Your realism has commanded both sides. The stubbornest realists found it true beyond their wildest preaching and formulas. What you gave them they could never have discovered but could always recognize. The poets flocked to you because your kind of truth was theirs; like them, you created a soul in reality.

Madame, your realism does not accept the surface of things and does not accept your own body, but forces these toward a more intricate and luminous expression of the life hidden within. Your realism begins with the pressure of life from within out, the permeation of the entire object with its spiritual actuality. And so in your art feeling becomes plastic, as if you were the sculptor of your own soul. One seems to see in your presence radiance, spirit, something like music and falling wind, a strange identity with trees and air and light. But at the same time one seems to hear the sound of the blood in your veins. Your words seem to come to us through your blood. The underlying, intense, and most urgent and beautiful precision of your art gives us the tremendous shock and quiver of life. And to such a realism as this, a formal or poetic art comes as natural as a gesture to a living hand; it meets no sudden break, but is a consummation of the truth that was present, though in a less degree, from the very start. From your Hedda Gabbler to your Francesca would be a continuous line.

Madame, you, of all artists in the theatre, know that, seen most deeply, life becomes a dream; there is so much of our own reality added to it that nowhere out of ourselves can it exist. And your kind of realism easily becomes mystical; it renders everything, and because it is so exact, so patient and so infinite can give back their mystery to things and make them like a dream again.

LETTERS FROM DEAD ACTORS

RACHEL TO PAULINE LORD

MADEMOISELLE—When I see you play, I am filled with remonstrance and envy, I as the great classical actress of France, you as the best actress in America for a certain kind of tragic realism.

You know my story, Mademoiselle. My father was a Jewish pedlar, a street hawker. I was four years old when my sister and I joined the troupe of Italian children that went wandering over the country singing in taverns and on the bridges; and my business at first was to go about and collect the pennies that fell to us.

When I was nine we drifted to Paris, and in the streets there I sang, a rough voice, but with such energy that the great Choron took me to his house and gave me lessons without charge. I studied at the Conservatoire, I played with no success, and at last I found a chance at the Comédie Française. Without applause I played Corneille's and Racine's heroines, until my Phèdre came and took Paris and from Paris spread my glory over the world. Kings flattered me, authors wrote for me, the Czar of Russia once

rose to give me his seat. It was I who stemmed
the tide of Romanticism that had arisen so hotly
ten years before my Phèdre. I gave new life to
the classical art of the French theatre. It was I
who handed on the tradition to the great Bernhardt. For fifteen years I triumphed continuously on the French stage until, in the summer
of 1858, when I was only thirty-seven, death
came.

My genius lay in the representation of great
tragic passion, love, malignant hate, rage and
consuming despair. My method was the classical; its track was elevated, with a kind of
open and universal simplicity in its tremendous
power. My voice, which was naturally harsh,
became, with long training and labor, most even
and secure in tone, and, in its quality, tragic
and penetrating beyond words. My pallor, my
voice, my body and all its motions, my silences,
seemed when I was acting to be universal. And
I set on all my art the stamp of the great style,
which was myself expressed with distinction and
magnificence.

To my classical school you, Mademoiselle, appear to reject style. I watched for it throughout your playing in *Anna Christie;* I watched
for it in *Samson and Delilah,* in *They Knew
What They Wanted.* Do you distrust distinction, Mademoiselle? It is all theory to you perhaps? Or have you no way of giving yourself any

grandeur, of setting free by means of your art something superb, something that comes off from the individual artist and goes on existing in the world like a great thought or pattern or idea?

In the second act of *Samson and Delilah* how dry and unheroic you were, sitting there in those exotic clothes of the East when you played the actress rehearsing her rôle of Delilah! How badly you read the verse! Do you mistrust that too, Mademoiselle, do you distrust the element of pure art added to the natural that poetry must be? Could you not see that convention in a work of art is only a way of giving to it its own life, of separating art from accident and nature?

I understand what must be your theory. If you had told it to me in my own day, I should have gasped. All this soiled, drab, back-alley detail, I should have said then, what has that got to do with art? It is not even romantic in M. Hugo's style, I should have said. Is art to be ash-barrels and hoarse servant girls, and gin and ginger ale, as in your *Anna Christie?* Is art to be things without taste or power or beauty even in their evil or mediocrity? But why so insistently flat, I should have asked you, Mademoiselle? How stupid, I should have thought, to see you standing there without grace or elegance or fire, to see you permit yourself so colorless a presence. My body was like a marble in which some god stood and which his power moved. I should have twiddled my fingers from the end of my nose at you and laughed—as I did to the grand marquise once, not meaning her to see me, alas, as she did!—but, though I should be a street gamine still, as I always was, I should be another matter when it came to art, and from the height of that I should have scorned you. That, of course, is how it was with me then.

But I am wiser now. I do not remonstrate with your theory of art, for I see now that all theories have their truth, that they are all voices of life, and that there must be some larger and more complete art in which all theories should have their place. And so now I can grant the theory of your school of acting. It is to represent in terms of repressed emotion all that is terrible in one's life. To concentrate in your body a bitter, mute violence. To get the effect by the negative; to speak by keeping silent; to move us terribly by what you do *not* do. There was a short moment in *Samson and Delilah* when you reached a summit under this method, the moment where you crouched near the table expecting to be killed by the frenzied poet whom you had betrayed. And, in *Anna Christie,* all during the first act, with the dramatic truth of its dialogue to supply your matter, you were wonderful, Mademoiselle. You had there, in your tragic eyes and your frail body and your haunted voice, all the store of your wrongs and your suffering, you were at that moment a great artist, you were secure, inevitable. But, later in the play, which, too, somewhat failed you after the first act, when the more positive emotions came and the pressure of a more immediate and violent life, you were not as good. What you do best so far is the backwash of violent passion, the after-mood, the parching tongue, the gray despair of that which is past but remains as a darker, inverted, inarticulate tragedy.

When later you played the little restaurant waitress in California, who married the husband so much older than herself, there could have been no one who did not admire your beautiful effacement of yourself among the players, no one who did not feel the sweetness and goodness created in the character everywhere and but half said, no one who was not moved and held by that voice that asks so little and asks so much. But I will not say that this is enough. Mademoiselle, though you may avoid my school and method of art, you should yet believe that —whether or not the expression of them in the theatre is eloquent and elevated and removed and classical—these elements of life are there, nevertheless, to be expressed. It is not what you believe, it is your denials that I object to.

You should admit more into your problem.
Get more range. Keep your strange, moving
voice, if you like, where there is need for it, but
cultivate more flexibility and less monotony of
tone for much of your speaking. Cultivate magnetism, Mademoiselle, learn to charge your body
with life when there is need of it; to make our
eyes follow it; to make it inseparable from the
dramatic moment it shares; sometimes your
body should be as negative and apart and plain-
tive as it is now; but your body should not be
always so; it should be the focus of all the life
taking place in you. Keep your theory, but admit more to come under it.

However you may choose to express your
matter for us, believe more in the flame of things
as well as in their ashes in the soul. Study for
that; you will never be a great actress, either
realistic or otherwise, until you know it. And
in your own school you will never be great until you know clearly one fact, which is this:
the great classical artist has to study his matter
till he finds in it some large, simple pattern,
some poetry of outline, that will convey its
truth and its infinite implications; but the realistic artist, though he expresses it in terms of
the actual, has also to find his main truth and
emphasis; and he needs as much style—in his
own kind—as the classical does, as much imagination, range, variety, and a more complex if

less elevated technical expertness, before he can find the truth.

Dear Mademoiselle, I envy you and your modern realists many of the things that you can do. The little homely nuance, the brutal ugliness, the domestic, the photographic, the gentleness of the common people, the sweetness of familiar images, the lives lived in shadow or dumb byways, the daylight and prose analysis, the endless range of observation and detail. I had none of these. My talent was not for them; my school of art disdains them. To me when I lived they would have seemed trivial and unworthy of an artist, seemed of the *canaille*. My art may have been greater or less than the art you follow, but it was different.

I could and would only represent those emotions which are general, not those minute and sometimes strangely sweet or homely or sordidly accurate feelings that you can show. I could grow pale or flush, I could rave or weep or curse or pour out an impassioned love, but I could not be gray or ashen or familiar; even my sorrow had to be splendid, and my grayness a wide despair.

My art was the heroic. The region of it was in those passions that shake the world and those forces by which men's lives are nourished and consumed. You, Mademoiselle, in your best moments can be like bitter tears long since dried but more bitter than ever; your art can be like a brittle, stunned, dumb echo of some former wrong done to your soul. My soul was like a cavern from whose darkness resounds the eternal voices of the wind and sea.

LA CORALLINA TO DORIS KEANE

I saw you, Signora, in *Romance*.

I said, "What a beautiful movement! It is like a swan! An actress who knows how to walk," I said, seeing your brave, lovely motion across the stage. I heard you take our Italian voice exactly; you knew how to whiten the vowels, how to sing the tone, how to get the staccato. I heard you laugh in your *Czarina*. I saw your clear, eloquent wrists. There, I thought, is an actress with intelligence; one sees that she has a brain that can direct her body to what her will is driving at; she can point, she can put her foot down; she is not limp and sweet.

Signora, you are the only actress in America that is like me. You are like what I was when I reigned nightly at the Sant' Angelo and Venice came to see me.

Our Venice then was the summer of the world. Nobility and fashion and culture came from over all Europe to our golden city. Venice understood the world of these, she taught them, entertained them. We had five times as many theatres then as Paris had; and two hundred cafés whose doors never shut. In Venice it was eternal day. There were candles burning in the theatres, at the opera, in the grand *saloni* where the card tables were, and in the ballrooms; on the canals there were lanterns and torches where the lovers set out for Venus' Isle, and everywhere burning eyes looked out through masks.

"La Corallina," Venice called me, though my name was Maddalena Raffi. The great Goldoni said of me that I was pretty and pleasant and had a marked talent for comedy. But that was in his memoirs, written when he was gray and eighty and his flame was cold. In those happier days he adored me, he haunted my steps; in sum he could not get me out of his mind, La Corallina.

And in that one season of 1751–52 he wrote for me seven comedies, in all of which I succeeded. One of these plays Eleonora Duse has since taken to every European capital: *La Locandiera* was mine. As the Mistress of the Inn my triumph was such that Medebac, my rival, the wife of the manager of our troupe, grew so madly jealous that Goldoni had to write another play in which she alone might shine. But, to close the season, he wrote yet another for me, *The Jealous Women,* and in that I came off with such brilliance that poor Medebac fell into convulsions. But that was not my fault.

Not only the Venetians but the French nobles lodging in the town, the Austrian princes and the great English lords, I dazzled with my playing. I knew the world because it came to Venice. I knew the cities of Italy, for I had played in them. Bologna had been at my feet, Signora, as London has been at yours. I had my paintings, my silver tea service from the Duke of Parma, my diamond patch box from the Conte Lodovico Widiman of Padua, my lace, my fans, my court. You may have heard of how a Dalmatian prince presented to me a monkey with a coral necklace which another lover, for no love of monkeys, changed to pearls. I looked out on the world with a warm, clear wit. And the world came to see me enact my great rôles. I gave them their life as I saw it. I gave them my comment.

Signora, when you played Catherine, I could not blame you for not expressing all you saw in the rôle. You had a public and a century that has grown middle-class and nervous about many matters. It mourns over these matters and whispers solemnly about them, or it is coarse and rowdy, but it is afraid to delight in using its wits about them. The masses have made people who ought to know better, forget that it is the play of the mind, and not the forbidden subject, that is the thing we rejoice in. In that American theatre of yours you have emotion, energy, sometimes serious thought; but you have very little pure mind and wit. Broadway should have come for a while to Venice, my dear, and made a little glittering sojourn there, but, alas, there was no Broadway then, only wide seas.

For such a public as yours Catherine and her ways of life would be raw meat, as our *Commedia* used to say. She is like the vindication of the nature in us all. She rips off too much veneer. She is aristocratic and barbarian at the same time; and neither of these can fit a bourgeois public. With a parterre of kings perhaps, or with M. Voltaire in the orchestra stalls—but why dream? Your brain understood Catherine very well and recognized her fantastic and comical magnificence. But you could have no hope of being free to express all you saw.

What you did in *Romance* was right. With most of your audience it passed for sentiment. They took it for the tearful story of a gay and unconventional prima donna who for love's sake renounced her own passionate love. That was the chief thing in the play for them perhaps, and people must get what they can. But you saw the story with your wits about you. You put the comedy into it by knowing it was tragic, and the tragedy by knowing it was comic. One saw how well you know that humanity is always a wonderful clown, sometimes superb, sometimes absurd, but always getting the stick on its back.

You knew that this *Romance* was the drama of passionate and abundant and wilful human nature forever welling up and forever being baffled, inexhaustible, hungry, and wild. You knew that this woman's romantic abnegation was only another piece of energy, and a lovable, vain search for the peace and solution that would never come. And so you found the truth by seeing the disproportion of this one soul to the conditions of life and by setting out the tragic humor of its wistful vivacity. And what you saw you had the means to express through the music and glitter of your technique.

There is already in America on the tragic side a simple feeling and form that may some day be great. In comedy there is a noisy, bubbling thing—very like the old improvised masks that Goldoni displaced with his comedy—that may come to something in time. But what your American theatre most often has is an infantile, sentimental comedy too silly to think of. Its appeal is nympholeptic sometimes, sometimes mildly moral, and always sentimental. This Syrup Comedy has its crowds. And many who are bored by it, are slow to sniff, perhaps because, as it seems to me, your Anglo-Saxon race has a respect for the mere absence of brains.

But you will never succeed at that game, Signora; you must let no prudence and no friendly advice and no long-run temptations push you toward it. You do not understand sentiment. You have a Latin mind. It is full of clear lines of wit, of daylight disillusion and the instinct for laughter. You have a kind of mystical and gentle fatality and absence. You have some of the austerity that comes of having made choices among ideas of living.

In *Romance* the lash of all this came out in your art. The precision of your beautiful romantic effects, when you played, showed a smiling mind hidden beneath them, but no sentiment. The right feeling was there, but, for those who could see, the wit also. You can never be the sort of every-day, lovable and whimsical character so dear to your public. Yours can be the comedy of distinction; or the comedy of the beloved romance of life that is lived in a rich frame; or of the trenchant worldly wisdom that tradition gives. Or you can express the comedy of a tragic and sharp mentality. In your America you have a public eager for more acting that can make a cosmopolitan criticism of life and can paint it for those who are neither adolescent nor doting. It seems there are people who have been sixty or seventy times and more to see you in *Romance*. But that, as you would say, is not so much: coming three times a week it is only twenty-three weeks or so. You felt a pleasure in that fact all the same, and I understand that too. You in your epoch travelled far more than I ever did, Signora, but you were the same when travelling. You liked to be given the keys of the city and then to find your retreat within your own secret, private mind.

Signora, what I did was to make my comment on the world I saw. I had no poetry beyond that of a keen and honest eye. I had imps in my brain that saw what men and women ran after or over which they were naughty and laughable rivals. I saw the irony in power, the passionate farcicality of love, and the vanity of to-morrows. I laughed because I liked to laugh and because there was nothing else to do when one knew the end of things. And I had an honest mind that hated shams and hypocrisies and knew on the stage how to hit them off.

I adored the theatre. Goldoni and I smiled at what Monsieur Voltaire wrote to our friend the Marquis Albergati about the theatre—it was, he said, "the most divine pastime that cultivated men and virtuous women can enjoy, when more than two of them are gathered together." I smiled at that, seeing how wicked and delicious it was; but I had the same adoration. I loved the audiences and the brave show they made; the Doge himself came and Caterina Loredan, and even the Infante Don Philip of Spain.

I wanted them to think that what I did was, for all its high spirits, a picture of things. I loved their laughter and applause. But what I loved best was my own mind. And that gave a sparkling and solid unity to everything I did.

DAVID GARRICK TO JOHN BARRYMORE

Sir: Great applause has come to your Hamlet, as it did once to mine. But, as I saw you, from the start to the finish of your performance, I understood more and more that you and I set out for this creation from opposite poles. So that what you have to do to perfect your creation is precisely the reverse of what I had to do.

At the beginning, my playing of Hamlet was irregular and vehement and pettish. But my performance improved almost nightly. At first I made Hamlet struggle violently with his friends when the ghost beckoned him. Later I made him remain awe-struck and motionless before the beloved spirit. At first I left out the advice to the players; I restored it later, though I always spoke it too pedantically. With Ophelia I was at first too rough and violent, with Polonius too rude. But these and other defects I softened and corrected, and at length perfected my conception of the part. Certain passages in my reading stood out always as affecting and sublime. When I taunted myself with a cowardly and pusillanimous heart, I swept the whole theatre along with me. When, by a sudden transition, I began to unfold my plan to catch the King's conscience, the house listened breathlessly. The horror and the terror of the ghostly visitation I expressed incomparably; I acted for the ghost. At the line

But break, my heart, for I must hold my tongue

I paused before the last word and dropped my arm to my side; then, with the force of the gesture, I spoke the word as if I could scarcely give it utterance. These and many other effects were universally admired. But to the last I kept some odd pieces of business, as when, for example, where Hamlet has to say that some must watch while some must sleep, I walked backwards and forwards twirling a white handkerchief in my hand. My performance was superb; but it continued always to be very vivid, very much underscored.

Sir, you began not with heavily marked passages; you began with no disproportionate accentuation, but with an outline already finished, distributed, even. From the moment the curtain rose on you sitting there, the picture of pale thought and brooding, dear loss, to the end, when you were carried by death and the strong arms of action up that flight of stairs and out beyond that high arch, you made of your idea one unbroken and complete line.

But one thinks not so much of any particular business of yours or any one scene, as of a distinguished continuity and taste. What you will have to do, then, Sir, reverses my necessity. You will have to fill in your design.

Sir, I erred—as I see now—and you err, in making this character and life of Hamlet too simple. Neither of us would admit it whole. My age, which was the age of Dr. Johnson and Sir Joshua Reynolds, followed close on the heels of an age of reason, of Mr. Pope and Mr. Addison, and the social philosophy of the French. To us Shakespeare's creation seemed no little barbaric, confused. And the graveyard scene seemed a vulgar muddle; I used to refer, indeed, to the rubbish of the fifth act. I cut that scene, left out the grave-diggers entirely. I altered the scenes with Ophelia and wrote in lines to make them more intelligible. I made the aspect of the character elegantly familiar, dressing Hamlet in the French fashion of the time, the black coat, knee breeches, the waistcoat with flaps; I wore my own hair. In sum, though I left the whole of it aristocratic and fine, I reduced Shakespeare's play to the thought of my century. You, Sir, have erred toward your democratic epoch. You simplify the play overmuch by making Hamlet too easy to understand; by putting him in terms too satisfactory to your public.

A part of your success is due to your presence and magnetism and to your capital achievements in playing. But a part of it also is due to your making Hamlet very easy to digest. Your audience of free democratic citizens feel that, for the first time, they understand what it all means. But, Sir, Hamlet is the dreamer, the human soul beating itself out against limitations, the scholar, prince, lover, wit, poet, clown, the mystery. And so he remains not real but, as it were, super-real. I see now that the very essence of Hamlet is that we could never understand him.

In your scenes with Polonius you were admirable. Most actors for the applause they get play up for all it is worth Hamlet's rude wit at the old man's expense. But you gave us only Hamlet's sense of the world grown empty and life turned to rubbish in this old counselor and Hamlet's sense that in Polonius was represented that special element in life that had robbed him of Ophelia.

Your many economies, Sir, were superb. The nunnery scene with Ophelia was done with a reaching out of hands almost; in the closet scene the relation of Hamlet to his mother and through her to the ghost was achieved by his moving

toward the ghost on his knees and being caught
in his mother's arms, weaving together the bodies
of those two, who, whatever their sins might be,
must belong to each other at such terrible cost.
About your performance there were none of
those accessories in invented stage business, but
only that action proceeding from the inner necessity and leaning on the play's life, not on stage
expedients. But if you would carry forward from
this first performance in the year 1922 the poetry
and mystery of Hamlet, you must create the
sense of a larger inner tumult, and indeed of a
certain cerebral and passionate ecstasy, pressing
against the external restraint of him. Your Hamlet needs the suggestion of more vitality, ungov-
ernable and deep, of more complex suffering, of
not only intellectual subtlety but intellectual
power as well, of the shy and humorous mystery,
the proud irony, the storms of pain. With your
fine, clear outline give Hamlet the nuance of
more shadow, more of a fitful magnificence,
more confusion, more inexplicability. And, most
of all, you must give to your creation more
poetry and richness of soul; there is lacking in
your art a fulness, a kind of noble generosity,
to make it spacious and profound.

Sir, the whole theory of an art of acting that
the Europe of my day held, was not that which
obtains in your generation. Under that theory
acting was fundamentally a separable thing

from the actor's state of feeling. Technique in itself was highly considered; sheer mentality played a conspicuous part in an actor's effects and the audience's pleasure. The test of an actor lay in his possession of a general talent, the ability to do all rôles with an equal truth. Toward this versatility the equipment of an actor consisted, first of all, of mimetic powers and of a face and figure capable of every variety of expression. And finally he required an intelligence that could build up out of reality an idea to be created.

For such an art I had every gift. In my first season I astounded London by acting with the same success Richard III, a rascally valet, a uxorious Puritan, a fop, a conceited author, and then in one evening King Lear and Master Johnny, a country lout. My mimetic gifts, my eyes, nose, mouth and voice, were such that I could pass through many characters and emotions in a few minutes, completely different in each. In the salons of Paris, where I was adored, I acted the dagger scene from Macbeth with overwhelming and tragic beauty, and passed from that into a cook's boy letting fall a tray of pies into the gutter. My body was in perfect proportion, and I seemed to be present in every muscle. My very presence on the stage had an air of life. I was, of all things, first an actor.

To your ears and your public such details of

physique and technical means sound merely external. Certes, if left so, they would be. But, Sir, never believe that I went no further. I knew the uses of these resources. I knew that the actor must have his idea and his effects prepared and ready. But I knew also that great acting could never stop there. I knew that from genius there must be the life blood that bursts forth and, like a flame, shoots through the spectators' veins. I knew that in the greatest moments in acting, the actor has the feeling of the instant come upon him unexpectedly. I testified that the greatest strokes of genius have been unknown to the actor himself till circumstances and the warmth of the scene have sprung the mine, as it were, as much to his surprise as to that of the audience. This I made the difference between great genius and good playing: good players give pleasure by their strong power and good sense; the great genius will always realize the feelings of the character and be transported beyond himself. It is this great and generous translation beyond yourself that you will most need.

Sir, your art, and the theory of art that your age maintains, are more private than mine, less social and general and separable from the personality of the actor. You have not so many of these external acting gifts as I had. You have an admirable presence, but you are not mimetic; your pantomime could mean little in itself. Your

body and your face are not eminently flexible
and expressive. Your features are incisive, delicate, significant, rather than mobile. Your voice
is admirable, but not yet a great instrument; it
is still something conscious of its training. Your
delivery of the verse is good but lacks somewhat
that resistant flexibility, to use an old phrase,
that is the soul of fine reading. You of all things
are first not the actor but the artist, yet you attain to beautiful acting. At your best, for your
performances vary in excellence from night to
night, you excel in what a painter might call the
fine drawing of your scenes, in the outward simplicity of your method, and your power to create
on the stage not so much the action of a drama
as the air of a compelling mood. But the fundamental principles of your art and mine remain
the same. Your business, as mine was, is to labor
toward finding in your art a language suited to
the finest reaches of your time.

MOLLY NELSON TO MARGALO GILLMORE

My dear Young Lady: I was an actress whose
name you have never heard and nobody among
your friends ever heard of me. I was born in
Louisiana, in the seventies, in a village not far
from New Orleans, of a Scotch father and a
French mother. When I was twelve years old
a company of actors came to our town for a

fortnight, playing *Richelieu* and *Romeo and Juliet* and a number of old-fashioned farces and melodramas. My mother and I went to see them one night, then the next night we returned and took my father. My father and mother after that, though they had enjoyed the play, would have stayed at home, for they were moderate and thrifty people; but I would go again; I cried all night; and they, to humor me, for I was an only child, took me again; and so it came about that every night I went to see that company of actors.

From that day I meant to be an actress. I said so to my parents and they laughed at me. They had already other hopes for me, my father toward my education and establishment in life, my mother toward marriage and a family. When I was older I spoke of it again; my mother wept, my father, who was a religious Scotchman and a tyrant, threatened, if I persisted, to turn me on the streets. At seventeen I considered myself a woman and announced my intention to run away, if I must, and join a company playing in New Orleans; and my father ordered me out of his house and sent my things after me. I never saw either of my parents again.

In New Orleans I found at last a chance to become an actress. My beauty and my eagerness made a way for me. The company I joined played sometimes in the city, but for the most part went barnstorming through the country, through Louisiana and lower Mississippi and into Alabama. The actors in it were mostly poor, stupid people without talent or ambition, a few of them through drink or bad fortune had come down in the world from better theatres. My success with my audiences was so great that almost from the very first I was given leading parts. I acted oftenest in the worthless plays of the day, which in the provinces were low indeed; for sometimes our company served not only as entertainment but as an advertisement for a patent liniment. In our travels to and from the towns we put up signs along the roadside, telling how our remedy cured sprains and rheumatism. In one play my old father was killed by a villain and I, dressed in a long green velvet gown, was obliged to end my great scene by saying: "Here, over the dead body of my father, I, Jean Ingleside, do swear to have my revenge." But the part I loved best was Juliet, which because of my beauty and romantic youth we played now and then. Even in the most miserable of these Southern places there was some faint glamour around highsounding names like Shakespeare's.

Meantime I studied continuously, there were plenty of books from the city; I kept to myself as much as I could, learning part after part, dreaming of finding my way to New York, of becoming a great actress and some day speaking to the world. But years passed, there was nobody to carry me out of the round that had caught me. I had only a country fame for my reward. And one night, long before I was thirty, I died of pneumonia, which I had caught going fifty feet through a snow-storm up an outside stair from my dressing-room to the stage in the hall where we were playing.

Dear young lady, I saw you in Andreyev's *He Who Gets Slapped*. In this play the part of Consuelo, the bareback rider, fell to you. She is young, simple, free, innocent, driven by her foster father to the arms of the fat baron; drawn, dimly, to Bezano, her partner in the circus. She is perplexed when He speaks, the philosopher who, when he had grown sick with the mediocrity and treachery of the world of men, has come to the circus to be the clown that gets slapped; and in the end she dies poisoned by him to save her from her fate. Dear young lady, you played Consuelo very prettily. You were dainty and innocent and fair; I watched you enter, and laugh, and listen when He spoke his wonderful lines about the goddess rising from the sea foam; I watched your terror of the disgusting fat suitor, your shy looking after Bezano. It was a very pretty little princess in a fairy tale that you played.

But what a part that was you had! Could

you not see what this girl was? The baron seeks her for a beastly purpose because he is a beast. Bezano seeks her as the woman for him; the circus people love her as the favored child among them; He, the clown, loves her because she is like his own dream. And Consuelo herself is the centre of the play, which turns on the theme of love. She is the thing itself, unconscious of what she is. She is all beauty, untouched by the world, complete in itself, seen only at moments, perfect, immortal. She should have been there on the stage the thing within life that all life seeks and that shines through all as a light shining through a restless and passionate dream.

Dear young lady, I worked. I used constantly to watch people's faces on the street and when they listened to music. And when I played in New Orleans I used to slip away sometimes all day and wander on the outskirts of the town till I came to the great cemetery of St. Roch. I used to wander in those avenues of vaults and under the dark pines and magnolias and through the box walks. There were many statues in the place, marble saints, images of Christ and his mother, angels and ideal figures of the dead. I used to walk about looking at these statues, stopping as if to visit them. I tried to imagine what they were thinking in such a long silence as they kept. Some of them I loved; and I tried to imitate their gestures. I tried to pour through my body the lines of a statue and, standing before it, to make my limbs, my head and arms and legs, alive with the same life as the life in it. I sought to gain for my body the unforgettable images that these marbles caught. When we were in smaller towns I used to escape to the country and walk hours, mad, lost in my dream, till twilight came down over the fields and over the water of the pools and I was obliged at last to hurry back to the theatre.

And then that night on the stage the thought of the country lying tranquil in the night air or of those marble figures standing there bowed or holding up their arms in the starlight, came over me and seemed the meaning of the eternal life beneath all art; and I could not go on; I stood speechless; and in that pause of silence I could feel a thrill run through my audience, and a moment later a thunder of applause came. What would I have given to have played this Consuelo! And to have played it in New York before an audience there, or in any of the great capitals of the world!

Dear young lady, I think of you in that rôle of Consuelo that fortune sent you, and of your prosperity in the theatre. And with you I think of other young actresses in New York whom luck has visited and who have taken so pleasantly these wonderful parts that fell to them. There is, for one example, Ruth Chatterton, who had Mary Rose to play. Barrie's piece is loose, is foolish in places and sentimental. But what a part Mary Rose would be, the girl, the dream in two worlds, called away by the spirits, drawn back years later to her son—the ghost of love, the eternal mystery! Or, among others, Jeanne de Casalis, who went so mildly through the part of Violaine in Claudel's *L'Annonce Fait à Marie*, when there was in it the gamut of love, pain and our endurance of every-day plain things and the sacrament of life and death and birth. What fortunate stars gave you young actresses these parts!

But I, who dreamed so and gave myself so to life, never had a chance. Nobody ever saw me who could do anything to bring me to good fortune. My audiences loved me more than they did my fellow actors because I was so real and shining and intense; but they took me without thought, merely for what I gave them, as they took the sun, the moon, human love, the coming of spring in the world around them. And, for all the world of men and art ever knew, I was no more than any of these things in nature that are thus taken for granted, and so I died as a chance love ends or the spring or summer passes, I who might have been, if any opportunity had ever allowed, a great artist. And so fortune in art favors some, and some are left to waste and drop out, unknown, lost, unarrived anywhere.

MLLE. BEAUVAL TO A TEA-PARTY
AT THE RITZ

Mesdemoiselles and Messieurs, I came to your tea, climbing down from Paradise not many more stairs than I had when I came from my attic in the rue St. Louis every night to go to the theatre. I saw at your party a charming company. There were ladies and there were gentlemen, every one charmingly, though somewhat expectedly, dressed. Some of you, no matter from where you came first to New York, appeared to be of a society truly urban; some were a little more like the provinces touched off with urban vulgarities.

Still it was an agreeable scene, such comfort and well-being and competitive complaisance, more chic than the angels I had left, but no less easy and secure from want. The apartment was warm as June in Avignon when we played there in the bishop's garden, though from your wide windows at the Ritz the snow and ice crackled outside over the roofs of New York. And how adorable were the flowers; their odors mingled with the ladies' perfumes from my dear Paris! And near by, through the tall door, was the glittering bath with its seas of hot and cold water, its porcelain and tiles and acres of towels; the Pompadour herself had nothing like it. And what chairs and lounges!

And to all this, to this room, with the summer there, and the flowers and cushions, rose the elevator in the hallway outside, sweeping your bodies upward from the earth as only, in my time, the souls of men, however great they were, could rise. It was not like my stair.

Meantime the conversation went on, newspapers, automobiles, Newport and many springs, trips to Europe—you all go to Europe or at least to Paris, is it not so?—clothes, gossip of the theatre, just the right breath of scandal, too, for the drawing-room, and a few whispered gutter dregs, and something now and then about the new players and the companies from abroad. I looked from one lady to another, one gentleman to another gentleman, and listened to what you said, finding it all most pleasant, I assure you.

But what troubled me, dear Mesdemoiselles and Messieurs, was this: I could not tell the artists from the others. I looked at the gentlemen without result. I looked at the ladies. Which were artists and which were not? I had thought there might be some look perhaps, something in the eye, some record of intensity, of pain, or joy or courage. Or there might be some precision of the features, or some bearing to go by. You, Messieurs, were all manly and agreeable, good traits for all men. And you, Mesdemoiselles, whether actresses or not, were one only more delightful than another. The dif-

ficulty was, Mesdemoiselles, I had never known
that the end of art was to approximate a lady.

But then, how should I know this: I was never
received into the society of my day in France.
Before I came to Paris to join the King's Company I was in the provinces. I was the adopted
daughter of Filandre, the manager of our company—only adopted by Filandre, I was actually
the cast-off child of some Dutchman.

You know what happened to us, you have
read all that in M. Scarron's *Roman Comique.*
We used to bump around in carts from town to
town, acting in tennis-courts, in rich lords' halls,
in hostelries and on the bridges. Some of us were
good artists, some were bad. There was, for example, little, dark La Racune, who if he had
been good to drink, would have filled hardly
two glasses, and so bad an actor that if there
were police to preserve the laws of the theatre
he would have been arrested nightly. On the
other hand, there was the divine Louis, who,
though he rode on a donkey, could spout as he
went the verses of Théophile's tragedy with such
style that the peasants we passed took off their
caps and crossed themselves.

You may have read how we came into the
town of Mans once with a cart laden with
trunks and packs of painted cloths that made
a pyramid on which I sat, drawn by a pair of
lean oxen and a breeding mare, whose colt ran

alongside. Destin walked beside me, as poor in habit as rich in mien, a patch over one eye and half his cheek, and with a string at his belt of crows, magpies, hens, and geese, like the spoils of war. And Rancour came behind, carrying a bass viol on his back and looking like a great tortoise walking on its hind legs. There were only these of us, the rest of the company was fled to Alençon from Tours, where our door-keeper had killed a soldier. Nevertheless in half an hour we were giving a play, Destin lying on a quilt and saying Herod's lines, and I playing Salome.

A fight in the audience prevented the finish of the play, it is true; but we recited grandly; even now in Paradise sometimes the lines ring in my ears. At that time I had a husband in the troupe, for I became enamored of Jean Pitel, our candle snuffer, and I dare say I married him. At any rate, time passed and all things happened. All dangers, every sort of glory. We played everywhere, inns, palaces, tennis-courts. We were cold, hot, hungry, rich, poor, in fortune and out. Ruffians captured our young women, barons and great ladies loved us, we found once a dead man under the bed. But we learned our craft.

At any rate, one fine day came the order from St. Germain. *De par le Roi!* His Majesty wishing always to keep the troupe of his comedians complete and to that end taking the best from the provinces, and being informed that the said Beauval— In sum, I went to the Palais Royal and Molière's company. I took up my abode under the roof there in the rue St. Louis. What triumphs were mine! And then the Duke took me up, and there was luxury. But though I lived richly and my art went on to greater triumphs, I still belonged to a world made up only of artists and gay adventurers and wild, brave nobles who went their own ways. I was only a player, and so I lived my life. I knew no ladies and I went to no great house. I never dreamed once of being a lady, though it is true I did dream of becoming a great artist.

But nowadays, Mesdemoiselles and Messieurs, it is so charmingly different, is it not? I do not see them among your company at tea, but there are no doubt artists who are less blest than you are, are more bitten and hurt, more set on learning a great craft. You will not need that craft. You may not know much, but you know a great many people and almost anybody might be you. I must be happy in seeing you on the stage as you are off it and seeing you do there what you do everywhere. Some of you had your torments and ambitions once, I dare say, but you grew quickly up into the general, and found in time your reassurance in success. It may be some one else's kind of success rather than one's own

kind, but, even at that, success in the Land of
Success is a great balm.

You come to the theatre. Your public have
had a busy day going in and out of places and
keeping as much like one another as they can.
They have been gathering their ideas from the
newspapers and journals, where you get yours.
They never hiss, they applaud with willing energy. You may well delight in pleasing them.
Let the foreigners, if they choose, abandon
themselves to theatrical outbursts and lose their
good practical sense, but not you. Sometimes
they too, if the cinema seasons favor them, learn
to play the game and manage so that their interesting faces look more sensible and vacant.

Hotel and country club and parlor car æsthetics and you, its obliging artists, more alike than
even the photographers and hairdressers could
turn you—the public that is yours is able to make
itself at home in art. The gutter has its violence
and its release from tense and cramped re-
serves; there are the schools of poverty, one-
night stands, reckless aspiration, loneliness;
there is the long labor by which a craft is got.
The people in vaudeville and in circuses must
reach some edge of vivid life; but I can look
you over as cheerily as one does the mildly artistic, mildly lustful and pretty covers on your
news-stands. In my day actors were not received
in society. In the eyes of society we remained

instruments for which it was not responsible but in which it saw expressed and enlivened the beauty and powers and desires of life. I can easily imagine myself understudying, as I did once in fact, Mlle. de Brie or even Béjart, but I should find it hard to understudy your department stores, clubs, teas, and social receptions. Mesdemoiselles and Messieurs, it is for an actor very often that a dramatist writes his play. Doubtless, some one here at your tea is writing plays that are fitted nicely to your quality. He knows exactly how far to go, what to put into his plays, and so all prosper together.

Yet you may be right, with your salaries, your apartments and suppers, your motors, cabs, social engagements, your gowns from the splendid windows, your good long runs and easy manners. In such a state of affairs an artist is free. He may do as any one does. And if your public would have you thus, who can blame you? If you express what they want expressed, what else is there to say, save that you are fortunate indeed in being able as artists to arrive at your summits in terms so simple as these? And meantime people applaud, and set one against another your interesting personalities, and strive to meet you and invite you everywhere. In a way, of course, it is flattering for them that artists should be so like themselves.

SEEING THE POINT

ONE of the commonest ideas about God is that no man could bear to look upon His face. The radiance there would be too great for mortal eyes. In an odd way the same is true of man with regard to all his experience—with objects, say, or actions or thought. He does not see the central light of experience, the essential quality that characterizes it and distinguishes it from everything else. He prefers instinctively to flee the point, to blur it over, to evade it, losing himself in a looser, easier, more elusive generality. The quality that he would willingly see in a piece of experience is a quality that may be called *a kind of a sort of a something*. And at the same time, by a yet deeper instinct, he is pursued by the essential, as he is by the idea of God; there is something in him deep down that waits for the fundamental characteristic to appear to him, to take him, to reveal the experience to him.

In art the average man is neither a poet nor a scientist; his perceptions are neither deeply poetic nor precisely realistic. He chooses a middle course which evades the point all round, giv-

ing him a little of every side without the inmost
sting and shock of any. He evades the sharp
comedy of things and he shrinks from their
tragedy; he chooses the sentimental course,
which softens, footlights and vaporizes a little
whatever it touches. With the experience portrayed he is too much at home to weep to the
last tragic bounds and too far from home to
laugh to the depths of humor. And yet at the
same time it is true, for example, that the plays
that hold him finally and that survive the whims
of mere seasons and single generations are those
that discover in their matter a great central pattern of idea and significance, and translate this
idea into all the dramatic elements involved.
The power of the artist and the completeness of
his performance achieve a concentration and
creative life that compel men to follow and to
make a great work of art a part of themselves.
Meantime, however, it is true, as Plato said, that
most men are blind to the fact of their ignorance
of the essential character of each individual
thing. They do not see in each thing that which
distinguishes it from every other; they do not
see what, if the thing were freed from all but
its own characteristic, would remain, and would
be the point of it, and would define its existence
in the midst of a multitude of things like and unlike. What men are least apt to do is to see the
point.

Every man has some ability and gift toward seeing the essential quality of what he experiences. He may easily see that the characteristic of a circle is a series of points equidistant from one point. The essence of a straight line is that it is the shortest distance between any two points within it. And from such as these he passes to more difficult pieces of experience, and to the discovery of what shall be for him the essential quality of the wind at night, say, or the poetry of Shelley or Leopardi, the art of Duccio or Botticelli, the character of a great city, of heroic figures in time, or cycles of thought.

An artist, however, is, by his very nature, distinguished from most men by the force that drives him toward an essential characteristic. The extent of this force is one of the measures of the artist in him. He approaches his material —the sculptor his living model or anatomy, the painter his landscape, the dramatist his men and events—and finds in it something that is his idea; he means to discover that element which for him will be the conscious being; he finds in his material that something; he finds that which will be for him permanent and ideal, and will remain for him when the material itself has faded. Out of his own substance the artist evolves forms, ideas, as out of the growing substance of a forest the tree form evolves, and then in turn the forest form from the trees, taken together among themselves. He is driven on to creation by his desire to free his idea from the confusions and accidents of the original material and to leave it essential.

The next measure of the artist's ability, however, will be the extent to which he can carry into the terms of his art the essential that he desires to express. Any one, almost, knows how easy it is at the start to get the outside. An artist often comes early on an external and accidental semblance of what he is attempting to create. With a little talent and less instruction or practice one may paint a pleasing landscape, trees, golden sky, birds flying, or make a pretty drawing. In music a beginner with a good ear and relaxed fingers can set up a remarkable effect. And a young sculptor can catch the outside of a head, find a nose and eyes and surface planes that make a highly plausible result. But only slowly does the young painter find his essential idea and the technique inevitable to it; only slowly the musician discovers the unescapable pattern of the musical form; and the young sculptor begins to be promising when he is unwilling to go farther than the point where he can actually carry into sculpturesque terms, into mass and line, into solidity of form, the head that he attempts. In the art of the theatre the nearness of the means—the actor, scene, and incident—to the material—men, places, and events—makes easily possible a certain semblance of an art. But to achieve theatricality, to discover in the material some fundamental point and at the same time to express that in the peculiar terms of the art involved, is far from easy.

The separate and individual nature of each art, and of any school or period in art, best appears through the essential idea or quality expressed in any piece of it. All arts have at bottom the same function and the same principles. But a like essential idea may be variously expressed in terms of the various parts of living, in mass and form, for example, or in color and line, or in words, or in an art that consists, as the theatre does, of light, words, places, and the movements, the voice, the bodies and presences, of human beings. The perception in a painting and in a statue, for instance, of such a like essential idea will make clear the difference between the expression of it pictorially or sculpturally, and so will in turn make clear what is essentially sculpture and what painting. It might make clear, also, how far or near to some particular experience that has been re-created in all of them the several arts may be, how available each one is for expressing the experience.

A company of artists are gathered together, shall we say, looking out over the sunset desert around the columns of Luxor. In the end the same necessity would hold for each of them, which would be to express some essential characteristic in the experience. Obviously the artist whose medium would most immediately convey the literal experience of the scene would be the painter. He, at his peril, may set down as much or as little of the actual scene as he chooses. The sculptor would have to remove the essential idea into some less representative or photographic form; what he derived from this experience might appear in the sheer relation of abstract lines and mass. The architect might give to the lines and spaces of a façade an essence which, in the art of words, a poet might call the serenity and austere infinity of that hour and scene. And the musician, dreaming of that desert space stretching forever away from the lines of those columns in stone, might express in the unknowable depths and forces of music a kind of inmost vitality in him at that moment. Meanwhile beneath all these several pieces of art there might be one essential characteristic of the experience in that time and place; and through the perception of this in its several embodiments in the various arts the essential nature of each art might be distinguished.

In the matter of the distinguishing characteristics of the several periods and schools in any one art, the same holds true. A like essential is expressed at various periods and in various schools. The expression of the idea of saint-

liness, for example, or of exaltation or elegance
might appear in Romanesque, Gothic, or Pal-
ladian architecture, and in Italian, Austrian, or
Spanish baroque. The theme of love appears in
Horace, Dante, Mallarmé and their followers.
The relation of individual impulse to the general
order and decorum is involved in Shakespeare,
Racine, Ibsen, or Morselli. From the perception
of the essential expressed so variously, the various natures of the several periods or schools may
be more clearly manifest.

In all arts the elements of beauty, style, and
purity have at bottom a pressing relation to the
perception of the essential quality.

In any experience beauty as a pleasurable at-
tribute appears when we perceive the characteristic quality and at the same time recognize
that in the experience this quality attains to a
certain unity and completeness. This is what
Saint Augustine meant when he said that all
beauty consisted in unity—*omnis quippe pul-
chritudinis forma unitas est.* In a work of art all
beauty derives from unity in its essential character; and however great a variety of qualities
may be exercised within this unity, every quality
is made to relate itself to this essential.

All style in art begins with essential idea.
When a painter says that another painter has
style, or when we say that Mounet-Sully had
style, we use the word in a somewhat special

sense. Style in that sense means a certain heightening, a certain added elaboration, something
that can be isolated from the content of the work
of art though it is not false to it. Style in that
sense is not necessarily the soul of the thing so
much as it is the lustre of the artist. But style
in any large and general sense comes back to
Buffon's remark that the style is the man, or
to Spenser's "soul is form and doth the body
make." Style is the medium by which the idea
finds expression. Style is what appears between
the content of a work of art and its appearance
in a form. Style is what arrives at that precise
point at which the work of art comes into existence. Before this point at which it achieves its
style, the work of art does not exist. In a work
of art the artist has a certain underlying essential idea or characteristic in the treatment of his
material, a certain point, which he sees as the
soul of it. This point he puts through every part
of it. Complete style arrives in a work of art
only when the idea is translated into the terms
of every part.

The difference between an artist and a man
who has intentions but cannot create them into
art, appears in the absence of the style that
might accomplish this translation of idea into
form. Minor artists and imitators, apart from
the significance of such ideas as they possess, are
what they are because they are able to put the

essential characteristic not through all the parts of a work, but only in this part or that. Mr. Paul Manship, beautiful and learned as his work may often be, has a statue of a girl with fauns that we may take as an example of such incompleteness. The turn of the girl's head, the lines and folds of her garment are in the manner of the early Greek marbles; the fauns, in the management of the ears, the nostrils, the little chasings to indicate the hair above the tail, the hoofs and the eyes, remind us of that lovely pair from Herculaneum, pseudo-archaic, exotic, charming past all words. But the girl's hands and her ankles and feet are almost modern in their character; in those two details the idea that characterized the rest of the work has not found expression, and they are therefore dead, and, in fact, never lived; they are apart from the rest of the statue, which is, therefore, only partially created.

Artists that are almost wholly eclectic and not very original get the form without the content. They learn from other instances of their art and from masters of it a manner of working; they take on bodies for which they have no fulfilling souls to contribute. They take over a style which says something not their own and is almost free of them. A highly eclectic sculptor, for example, may get the surface, the external manner, the character that he has derived from another, but he cannot get the essential sculpturesque solid-

ity which derives from the true relation of the
modelled mass to its idea. And it may happen in
all arts, also, that a style gets fixed, outstays its
meaning; the form remains, but half the fundamental idea beneath it is lost; as at the Théâtre
Français, for one illustration, where much of the
tradition is, at the hands of bad actors, lacking
in idea; or as in some of Michelangelo's followers, who got only his mannerisms without the
ideal necessity behind them.

No style at all, then, to repeat, can arrive until the artist gets the point, the characteristic.
The completeness of the style—and of the work
of art—depends on the extent to which this characteristic extends through every part. An actor
creating Œdipus can learn from the play itself
the character of every detail confronting him.
He can discern, for instance, that his make-up
requires a beard, and the obligation for a beard
will serve to comment on his whole problem.
That he must wear a beard the actor knows not
so much from tradition as from every separate
aspect of the drama. To begin with, the very
story itself is not personal with Sophocles but
was a racial myth ready to his hand. This story
—and the final form of it that he uses in his
play—consists mostly of outline, a large, general pattern in which the shadings of incident,
character, and emotional and ideal reaction are
included. The characters themselves are, first of

all, types, large forms, and afterward more or
less individuals. The emotions and ideas are not
so much personal as typical, powerful visitations
within these human vessels of forces larger and
more lasting than they, passing through them,
shaking and revealing and leaving them. The
images created, the diction employed in the
play, are kept within the bounds of a certain
size and a certain pattern of simplicity. From
all this the actor learns, then, at the very start
that his own features will too greatly individual-
ize the rôle; just as in turn he knows, in so far
as he is an artist, that the reactions he expresses,
and the gestures he employs must have about
them a certain outline quality, a pattern of universality; and just as in turn he knows that in his
recitation he must strive for line forms rather
than words and phrases, and so must move
toward a sonorous and impersonal and formal
manner of delivery. Sophocles as a dramatic
artist succeeds and attains greatness by reason
of the fact that the characteristic quality is carried greatly and completely through every part
of his drama, the story, the ethical theme, the
characters, the reactions, the imagery, diction,
the verse. His play possesses an absolute totality
in style.

The defect of Euripides, on the other hand,
great poet and dramatist that he is, consists, in
so far at least as the Greek dramatic form is con-

cerned, in his not being able to create or to introduce a style that could express his quality am-
ply or completely; Euripides leaves no little of
his thought and content undramatized, uncre-
ated, and conveys it to us as more or less separable moments of literature or philosophy; it
is as if Velasquez in his *Surrender of Breda,* instead of carrying into his very brush and into the
outlines of his forms the quality that in the art
of words we should speak of as gracious and
most suave, had attached written words to the
canvas to express further the idea in his mind.

In many a production of *The Merchant of
Venice,* the casket scene has had a mass of gild-
ing and tricking out, with every sort of detail,
cushions, canopies, throne-chairs and costumes,
coming and going, everything but the point;
which visually is the relation of the caskets to
the suitors, to Portia and to the whole scene;
which orally is the poetic rhythm and imagery;
which in sum is the pattern of idea, picture and
sound that underlines the scene. In the Hopkins-
Jones-Barrymore production of *Hamlet,* on the
contrary, the scene where Hamlet comes upon
the king at prayer was acted with the king on his
knees near the front of the stage, his hands lifted
to heaven. Behind him stood Hamlet with his
drawn sword in his hand. The two figures, one
behind the other, the lifted hands, the sword
pointing, expressed for the eye the exact pattern

of the scene's idea, the precise theme of relationships. Visually, at least, the essential of that
scene had been achieved, and had been freed of
every characteristic not its own.

An actor, therefore, is an artist only in so far
as he can first see the point or characteristic
quality and then put this through every detail
of his performance. His manner, his gestures, his
walk, his diction and quality of mind will differ
in *The School for Scandal* from what they must
be in Ibsen's *Ghosts;* in Regnard's play of *Le
Légataire Universel* he will eat grapes, make
love, wear his clothes or fight a duel in a style
that differs from his necessary style in Beaumont and Fletcher as Regnard's precision and
swift cold elegance differ from the gallantries
and lyrical whimsies of the two Elizabethans.
And it is through this principle that the actor
will know how to approach the question of
naturalness in acting, and to dispose of the usual
nonsense on the subject. He will know that in
acting, as in any other art, the only naturalness
there can be is in relation to the essential nature
of the work of art which he has in hand.

All purity in art begins with the translation
of the essential idea. A work of art is pure in so
far as it compels the ideas within it to stick to its
own terms; it is pure in so far as the ideas within
it find expression solely in these terms, without
relying on anything else. In a work of art that

is pure the idea—and every manifestation of it
—discovers a body that is free of all characteristics not those of the art employed. A painting of a majestical scene or of some heroic and
austere vista is not a painting at all—however
stirring it may be as a visual memory or as poetry
—unless this characteristic that, in the art of
words, we call magnificent austerity exists in the
color, the line, the brush, the composition of the
picture. And so with music and every art. And
that purity which we discern in the great artists'
natures—and to a lovable extent in most minor
artists, too—and in great saints, arises from this;
what they dream and desire is for its own end
and perfection, free of considerations outside
itself and untouched by the intrusions of another world of aims. For them the idea or dream
can alone be important; and by the side of it
they are not even aware of "all other idle and
unreal shapes attendant on mortality."

Criticism of art that is a matter of personal
preference and individual taste and private re-
sponses is not without value, however variable
these may be. But the aspect of criticism that is
most constructive, useful, and not to be debated,
is that which arises first from the critic's ability
to perceive the characteristic quality underlying a work of art. He abstracts this characteristic from whatever embodiments of it may be
apparent; he carries it to some ideal completion,
and then judges the work of art by this ideal,

by the extent to which this complete realization
of its idea is achieved. Where the critic can do
this he transcends individual accidents of mere
choice. And no small part of his cultivation will
derive from his training in the perception of and
the acquaintance with many characteristic qualities.

And, finally, in every man the delight and
happy nurture of all art—as of all other experience—will depend at length on his seeing the
point, on his discovery of the last necessary characteristic. With the growth and cultivation of
this faculty he will go learning to see the point
of what he considers and exercises himself upon,
taking a kind of delight in finding what seems
for him to be the soul of the thing observed.
From the body of it the essential idea emerges
like a soul; from the circle its circularity and its
perfect cessation within itself; from the moon-
lit plain what in language he calls its stillness
and infinite peace, the dream of it that there are
no words to describe; from the rose its roseness,
by which it lingers in the memory; from Mo-
zart his quality, and from El Greco his; and from
the poet of the *Eclogues,* the *Georgics,* and some
of the *Æneid,* that character of poignant and
lyrical reflection and ornate quietness that we
call Virgilian. These essential qualities of things
emerging out of them take on a permanence in
the man's life that seems to survive them, and to
achieve a kind of constancy; and so, out of the

flux of all things, to offer to us something immortal in mortality.

Through this development in a man it may come to be that his pleasure in a work of art does not depend so much on the discovery of superlative instances and hot enthusiasms often soon past. It relieves him of the sense that he must acclaim the work of art as the best in the world or the best he has ever seen; and allows him the pleasure, always possible, even in an inferior thing, of discerning what the essential quality within it is and the extent to which this quality has been expressed. And in his own mind at least, if not always in the work of art, these essential ideas may dilate themselves toward perfection. This will add to that development and perfecting within himself of conceptions, qualities, essential ideas, by which not only he understands art but he lives as well. From them he gets light for his own experience, and out of his experience he adds elements to the sum of them. Art becomes—as the rest of life is—the field for his immortal search and continuity. And through this, art can reveal those in whom life is a passion of oneness and duration; and can, as Plato said of a certain music, from the divinity of its nature make evident those who are in want of the god. In great art a man seeks, even more than in his own flesh, a body for that which he most wishes to preserve in himself.

THE ART OF DIRECTING

IN THE course of stage history the director has borne a varied name and a more varied relationship to the theatre. He has sometimes been the owner of the play, sometimes an actor from the company, sometimes the régisseur, or director of the entire production in all its parts, sometimes the producer or actor-manager. But whatever the problem of the régisseur, or producer, or actor-manager may be elsewhere, in our American theatre at present the director is the man with the script in his hand who stands behind the whole performance of the play, who, to varying degrees, prescribes what the interpretation shall be, what the actors shall do, and trains them how to do it. He is the *maestro*, the coach, the general behind the rehearsals.

The director is the artist who takes the drama as it is put into his hands and labors to recreate it in his own technical terms. And this drama, when it is re-created into these terms, becomes theatre and something that is different from what it was before. Directing is an art or it is nothing.

137

There is no such thing as a play directed exactly as it is written any more than there is a landscape painted as it really is. In any art the material that goes to make up the work suffers a change before it becomes this work, and this change, this something added, derives from the artist working. In Corot's *Ville d'Avray* the material was the landscape of trees, atmosphere, and light; the medium was the paint. In Houdon's *Voltaire* the material was a body and the character in that body; the medium the marble. The dramatist's material is men, life, experience; his medium the dramatic form. In the art of the director the drama itself is the material, and the actor in the midst of the audience and the designer's décor is his medium. It follows that when a drama emerges from the hands of the director it has undergone a restatement of itself, a translation into the terms of the theatre, and the importance of the thing added will measure the importance of the director.

Most directors are not distinctly one type or another; they belong in the middle ground between two extremes. But at one extreme in directing is the virtuoso. He takes the play into his own hands and does with it what he chooses, twists it, makes it his own. He may go the limit in violating its quality, in forcing it to his own ends.

At the other extreme is the director whose aim

is to carry out entirely the dramatist's idea. If the play is bombastic he makes his rendering of it bombastic, where it is cold he will be cold, where it is barren he keeps it barren, and so on; he covers nothing, he tries to discover and to restate in theatre terms the play's essential character and the style that expresses this character; to every element in the play he means to give its special quality and intention.

Both these types of directors are artists. If one appears more sharply than the other to be an artist, it is not because of his method, but because what he creates is better or worse. It is a difference in degree, not in kind. We may admire a performer who tries to play a concerto as closely as he can to what is written rather than one who sweeps it out of itself to his own mood and will. But in the end what finally decides the question as to whether or not either of the performers is an artist is the thing created. With Liszt, Schubert may become not only the material that Liszt interprets but also the material from which he creates something violently his own. The virtuoso director at his peril does what he wills in directing a play. He may be a good artist or a bad, according to the result that he creates, but he is an artist. The result must judge itself. The original drama may almost disappear before such a director has done with it, but, conceivably at least, we may be willing to forget it in order to possess the new creation. In the theatre the trouble, however, with the virtuoso lies in the fact that there will always be few directors who have as much to give us as have the plays that they direct.

Great talents like Gordon Craig may do what they like with a play, and risk the outcome. Gordon Craig might take *Othello*, for example, and change it into what, as a whole, it but slightly could be, or read into it something that it scarcely contains at all, and yet create for us a result magnificent in itself. Or he might lift one element in the play to an importance out of all proportion to the whole of it, and by doing so illumine and dilate forever the region that *Othello* can express. A dozen Gordon Craigs bringing to bear on Shakespeare's tragedy this radiant distortion and dilation in twelve different aspects might increase twelve times *Othello's* radiance and scope· But Gordon Craigs are rare; and for the most part we are apt to feel that any one so determined to say what he has to say rather than what the dramatist intended, should let the play alone and write another for himself. That seems only fair all round.

The kind of director at the other extreme from the virtuoso would by some persons be rejected entirely as a creative artist—to use a phrase that is often heard but that makes no sense, since an artist is an artist only in so far as he is creative.

We may take, for example, an orchestra leader and his rendering of a Beethoven Symphony, and a director and the play he presents. In each case what comes to the artist is already established, something is already created. The score is ready to his hand. Into it the artist, working in his own terms, strives to create life and thus to express what there is to be expressed. But even if every instrument in the orchestra rendered exactly the score written for it we should still not have the symphony created. Not in nature, ideas, or art is there any truth that is ready and expressed and is invariably the same; it is restated in every man that experiences it, and as significantly as the observer that restates it is significant. No director can give us a play as it is, however faithful his intention may be and however great his ability to carry out his intention. His ideal may be a fine one; he strives to disappear and to leave the play exposed and expressed, to achieve a style that is an invisible medium, like a laboratory glass that reveals the delicate processes of an experiment. But he remains the artist by whose creation this style and revelation may arrive.

MUSIC AS A BASE

The relation among a play's ideas, remarks, events, and emotions, how they follow one another, how they dispose themselves together and so reveal the whole meaning of the play, is expressed, in so far as concerns their precise meanings and definite points, through words and actions. The exact observations that Hamlet has to make on his own failure in the power to act is expressed when he says:

"Why, what an ass am I! This is most brave
That I, the son of a dear father murdered,
Prompted to my revenge by heaven and hell,
Must, like a whore, unpack my heart with words,
And fall a-cursing like a very drab,
A scullion!"

When we see Pirandello's hero daub paint on his face and put on the robes of Henry at Canossa, we know exactly what theme and disguise his plan has followed.

But these are more special and particularized elements of a drama. Beneath them lies the main body of the play. In the whole of it there is the emphasis of one part compared with another; the mass is stressed heavily here and lightly there, according to its importance in the whole. One speech leaps out from another, propelled by the inner conflict beneath them. One speech is distant from those near it because it arises from meditation in the speaker or from his continuous habit of thought. One speech is ready in the speaker's heart before the thing it seems to answer has been said, its lips were on the other's lips ere they were born. The pulse or beat of a line or a speech or a scene is here quick, there slow; the emotion or thought exhilarates, it retards. All these are a matter of pure relationships. Beneath the particular situation, the particular thoughts, reactions, deeds, every play can be reduced to this abstract basis. Every play has this abstract pattern of values. On this side it is for the most part closely connected with the art of music. A director can best study the layout of a play as if it were a musical composition.

Music, as every one knows, is of all arts, except architecture perhaps, the most ideal. That is to say, music does not involve imitation or concrete instances or definite concept; its region is pure to itself. Music is the beautiful eternity, the idea, the essence, the general quality. In sum, to take an example, where Hamlet can only say to us,

"But I have that within which passeth show,"

music can put us into the very state itself out of which this poetry or our tears arise. But saying that, of course, is a commonplace about music.

In the play the matter of emphasis, themes and characters and events, the speed, the vocal tone, rest all fundamentally and essentially on a base of music. The relation of the stream of points equidistant from one point is a part of the truth of a circle, an abstract thing. The height of a tower is a part of its idea. The quiet of the vowels and the contemplative measure in one of Virgil's pastoral verses is as much its truth as is the precise thing said in words, and to forget this is to forget the nature of art. To forget this is like saying that a madness to kill is expressed or conveyed in a remark stating, "I am going to kill you," rather than in the eye and the onward rush of the murderer. The length, the beat, the duration of a speech in a play are a part of its idea. The time between two speeches is a part of their meaning. The tempo at which a cue is taken and the tone of the voice are as much—and often far more so—the truth of a speech as the more exact and limiting words that are said. When Othello says:

"Never, Iago. Like to the Pontic Sea,
  Whose icy current and compulsive course
  Ne'er keeps retiring ebb, but keeps due on
  To the Propontic and the Hellespont;
  Even so my bloody thoughts, with violent pace,
  Shall ne'er look back, ne'er ebb to humble love,
  Till that a capable and wide revenge
  Swallow them up."

the main truth of the outburst, the sheer fact that it is an outburst even, is conveyed by a tremendous current in the declamation, by the vocal tone and flood of sound rather than by the special concept in each and every phrase. And unless this outline and rhythm are established, the speech breaks down into something of forced images and elaborate or even false details.

When Marchbanks, with the poet's insight, says to Prossy of the arid, hot heart and bitter, drab profession, that he can see nothing in Morell but words, pious resolutions, and asks if it is possible for a woman to love him, and Prossy, after trying to evade the question, says,

"Yes,"

it is obvious that except for her mere acknowledgment of a fact, the whole moving truth must lie in the time she takes before she speaks and in the tone of her voice. When Miss Clare Eames acted the part it was almost wholly her musical sense that made this particular moment in the play so mordant and touching. The Hopkins production of *The Deluge*, very interesting in its intention, wore out long before the end, because in this situation, where a group of people, shut in by the flood and faced with death, show reformations and candid fires not usual with them, and later, when safety comes, revert to their daily selves, the more or less dramatic repetition in the scenes depended for its point on a variation in tempo which was not achieved. And, finally, in the case of individual actors it is their time-sense, their sense of the exact moment for a cue, a speech, an answer, that does as much as any-

thing else to engage the audience's attention with
its constantly fresh vitality and surprise.

VISUAL MUSIC

There is an element, of course, in the performance of a play that speaks entirely to our
eyes. When the director begins to consider the
expression of this aspect of a play he may wisely
study every part of it as a set of pure relationships, a kind of visual music. He can study a play
as he might a symphony to discover what the
essential idea may be, and those groups, motions,
positions that will most help in expressing
through the eye what the other dramatic mediums are expressing through our other faculties or
channels of perception. He can define those lines
and masses on the stage, and then subordinate
what is secondary and omit some of the confusion
of empty or extraneous movements. He can study
a scene for its last, fundamental idea or characteristic and try to find what line, what visual quality,
will most express the essential idea of the scene;
and can employ that line as something in itself
expressive. And he can seek to establish what
is most important of all these: the visual continuity of the scene, its living rhythm in our
eyes, from the time it begins till it ends.

THE DIRECTOR'S MEDIUM

Granted a clear or important idea for the play that he will present and the means and ability to carry it through, the director has still a problem like that of any artist, who for the prosperity of a work has to consider what tact and judgment he will use to achieve the right relationship between the work and the public. There is a point beyond which if an artist carries his idea he will lose the sympathy of his public and so defeat his own end, which is to express his idea to them. On the other hand, too much consideration of his public may prevent the artist's going far enough to reach the point at which his idea will get itself expressed. In every art some concession, obviously, is unescapable; music, for instance, has to be loud enough to be audible; the musician must concede that much at least to his public. But in general as an artist you may choose to trim your sails in order to arrive at your wished-for port, or you may choose to miss the temporary destination or success and instead to stretch the bounds of your art, to chart new seas, to sight new forms, new possibilities for expression. You take your choice at your peril and according to your own nature.

But the artist directing in the theatre has to remember that the theatre essentially is an impure medium. It consists not only of what is on the stage but of the audience in front. The director will have to make an imaginative choice and proportionment of parts, so as not to leave out the audience from his creation. However prophetic or illuminating the stage end of his creation may be, if the audience is not rightly involved in it the creation suffers, as might be the case with a pianist who insisted on pouring water into the instrument for the sake of some future aquatic scale, but failed of any sound or anything besides his strong idea or inspiration. The director has to consider what effect he most seeks, what is the truth that he would most express. When this is found he must relate every detail to it, taking his choice as to how far he is creating for a complete present moment and how far for future innovation or extension. A thing admirably right in itself may, when the audience sees it, jump out of the frame and distort the whole picture. An unwelcome detail, however true in itself, may either wreck the truth of a whole scene or send it to a thrilling pitch. To say what has never been allowed said on the stage, what has been more or less banned as crass or outrageous, may swamp the play or may double its expressiveness. The director may take whatever chance he likes, but he has to work in all the elements of his art—the play, the actors, the audience.

RESTATEMENTS OF PLAYS

When a play is new, hot from the author's forge, it may be taken as written for its own time, its idea is stated for the dramatist's own generation. The director's business is an interpretation of it in theatrical terms. But when there is a play to be revived, a few years or some centuries from its birth, the director's problem takes on another shift in restatement.

In so far as a play was ever a work of art it was a living thing. Within his dramatic form the dramatist has arrested and found a right body for a section in the stream of life. Life may be said to rise and to fill for a moment such a form. But the very essence of life as distinguished from the dead is this streaming, this ever-changing current of it. The living content, no longer wholly arrested in this form, goes on with its stream and is not to be distinguished from it. The form without the content is empty and dead. In the history of an art the process toward degeneration, and through and past that to a new summit of excellence, a new epoch, consists of two courses: First, there is the survival of the form with less and less of the sustaining life that once brought the form into being; this is the so-called decadence of an art. Second, there is the progress of a new quality of life in need of its body and moving toward a form that will contain and express it.

In Euripides's *Bacchæ*, Dionysos, the god of ever-springing life and enthusiasm and ecstasy, could not be bound; prison-bars, fetters, no obstacle had power to hold him fast. Only the forms of his own passion and of his own thought and his own motion could contain his divine life.

Pirandello, for the modern theatre, has dramatized this idea. The theme in Pirandello's work is the dualism between Life on one hand and Form on the other; on the one hand Life pouring in a stream, unknowable, obscure, unceasing; on the other hand forms, ideas, crystallizations, in which we try to embody and express this ceaseless stream of Life. Upon everything lies the burden of its form, which alone separates it from dust, but which also interferes with the unceasing flood of Life in it. In *Henry IV* this man who has taken on Form, a fixed mask in the midst of changing Life, remains in it until the moment when his passion and despair and violent impulse send him back into Life. But only for a moment; the impetuous violence of the Life in him expels him into his masquerade again; in his tragic struggle between Life and Form, Life is defeated, Form remains.

To many a play, when it is revived, comes such a fate as this. The life in the play is defeated, the ironic form remains.

The performance of a play at the director's hands is not a mere matter of the written text.

Its truth can arise only from the combination of this text as it stands, plus the audience for whom it is given. In so far as a play is alive the living element in it is an impalpable, onrunning, delicately perilous reality on which an illusion of permanence has been imposed by its form. The life in *Macbeth*, for example, seems to be permanently expressed by the play as we read it, and this might seem to hold true even for its performance. But this, in fact, is not the case. In such a performance there might be academic phases of interest. As history of literature, as drama, as Shakespearian tragedy, it might, if you choose, possess an interest. But such kinds of interest, though studious and engaging, are apart from the play's vitality as art. And this is just the point at which we need most the director's imagination, need the genius in him for re-creating the play in the necessary new terms.

That side of Shakespeare's *Macbeth* that is a living thing, that speaks to the life in us and arouses a response from it, and fecundates and increases the volume of that life, must be restated in every revival—and in a sense, indeed, at every performance—of the play. The life in this play is not a fact, it is not a fixed and permanent statement; it is an ever-changing reality, unconfinable, a ceaseless flux, but real. The sixteenth-century *Macbeth* of Shakespeare derives from an earlier and more primitive base. It has beneath it such an element of shock and terror as is to be found nowhere else in drama. This primitive quality Shakespeare restated in terms of the morality and the complex style of his own Elizabethan age, and lo, we have his *Tragedy of Macbeth*. And now, in turn, this primitive quality and this Elizabethanness must be restated for us. Even if a director could discover every fact, every piece of business, exact reading, gesture, tone, of the first production of *Macbeth*, and could reproduce them for us to the last jot, he would not necessarily convey to us the life in the play. He might give us only something beautifully curious or antiquarian or historic, exhibitions in facsimile, but not *Macbeth* and its meaning to us. No, his business as an artist is to discover a rendering for *Macbeth*—which is his material—through his medium—which is first the actors and the décor of his theatre— to discover a rendering of such a kind as will restate for the audience present the significance of the life of the play. There is no right way to produce *Macbeth*. It would be a comfort to think so, to have something to rest upon, just as some right way of living would be a comfort. But with life and with art the same thing holds: the essence of being alive is a constant, perilous choice and a constant projection of imagination into living forms.

A part of the truth of a Greek play is its dis-

tance from us in time. To be alive it has to be
restated for us somewhat as its original material
had to be restated in it. For us a part of a Greek
play's truth is its Greekness, with all that that
may mean for us. In Restoration times a gentleman often carried a little bowl of gold or silver
which he could take from his pocket and rest on
the arm of his chair, and into it from time to
time might spit. Molière's gallants were merely
smart when they took a comb from their pockets
and arranged their curls as they sat in a lady's
salon. But the director who wished to give us the
quality of gallant gentlemen in his revival of
these social comedies could not show us such details, they would defeat his ends and give us not
elegance but only ugliness. These are simple instances, but they illustrate the case. What in
these particular instances needs most to be conveyed is the living thing, the permanent idea in
them to which we respond—in sum, their elegance. At whatever cost, this must be created or
the moment is empty.

The director's revival of a play, then, is a form
of creation, and in so far as this is not so the
play lies dead on the stage, a mere fact, the
empty shell where once there was an engaging
life. All compromise, change, or emphasis in a
new production of an old play can have but
this one end, which is in a way to keep it alive.
The extent to which the director preserves

closely the play in its original shape, or violates or distorts it, re-creates its essentials in new terms or even forces it so that we hardly recognize it for the same play, may affect the success of his enterprise, but it does not alter the principle involved. There are as many ways of doing *Macbeth* as there are generations of human life; and in its production the perpetual creation of a right body to express its truth is the condition on which alone *Macbeth* is kept not merely a matter of culture but a thing that in our experience is alive.

USE OF THE ACTOR

When the director, as an orchestra leader might, has achieved through the actors under him the desired emphasis throughout the performance, the time values, the tone, and so on, he remains to be considered as any artist in general would be who is making use of the means at hand.

Of late years there has arisen in the theatre a type of directing that proceeds on the basis of letting the actor alone. Up to the point of collision with the other players the actor can go his own way and almost unmolested in creating his rôle. The principle is to get good actors and let them go ahead. Up to a certain point this policy has worked. But it has been a limited and often fatal method. Provided you get good actors, and in cases where only one or two actors carry the whole burden of the scene and can, perhaps, work it out between the two of them, you may succeed. But in general the scheme is almost as hopeless as turning a crew of sailors loose without an officer to run the ship. And, moreover, this method leads to a relaxation and laziness in the director himself.

The other extreme in directing actors is an older and more tried policy. In it the one hand controls everything and everybody involved in the play, and not only controls the actor but dominates his conception of a rôle and the entire playing of it. Such a director at such an extreme may even give the actor the tone, the gesture, the movement. He may, when he likes, make the actor an imitation of himself. Up to a certain point this method also has often worked. If we must choose, it is on the whole safer than the opposite extreme. Provided the director himself has ideas that are capable of making the play into something worth-while, and has the force or control to work the actors into his will, he may succeed. And the discouraging inferiority of the mass of actors seems to argue for such a tyranny. But it obviously throws away no little of the individual resonance of the actor. And it tends to mechanize actors and to make them stale. It gives them stage tricks where real invention is needed; it leads them toward a more or less passive exploitation of themselves.

The necessity of the second method, the one controlling head for the performance, is plain. The whole scale of the play finally depends on that. The good element in the first method, the hands-off-and-let-the-actor-do-it school of directing, consists in the fact that at its best it allows the actor freedom to create and the possibility of succeeding in himself, of happiness in his own soul. It leads him toward becoming a better and better medium in which the director may work. The ideal directing combines the two methods.

But of the actor as medium there is more to say. As the medium in which the director works, the actor may be thought of somewhat as paint is thought of for the painter or marble for the sculptor. In every work of art the artist takes his material from nature or experience and translates it into his medium, creating in it, as he works, something that was not there before. His creation is partly in terms of his material and partly in terms of the medium employed. Our consciousness of the medium is a part of our perception of a work of art and of our pleasure in it. One among the many reasons why Velasquez is a great painter lies in the distinction with which the paint itself is a part of his work: the texture, the brush, the density of the painting-medium and the color as well are a part of the idea that Velasquez's picture presents. In Shakespeare, at his best, along with the dramatic emotion and the thought we have always a sense of words being employed, of sheer phrasing and diction, as a part of our delight. In the same sense a portion of the truth of an Egyptian statue lies in the granite of it.

In the director's use of his actors it ought to be true that the more he can use in his scheme of the play the actor's own stuff, the better. The different truths of a great sculpture in wood and a great sculpture in marble will consist partly of the difference between wood and marble. It ought to be the fact that a certain deepening in the truth of an actor's contribution to a play will derive from the actor's getting his results in terms of himself, making up out of his own elements the result that he creates. It will allow a better chance for those explosive accidents that we call inspiration, those moments when the actor is carried beyond his own plan or clear intention. At such moments a certain unexpected contribution to the director's creation may come from the medium itself, which may contribute to his invention, give him an idea. Many an architect has got a design, a motive, a form, from some quality of texture, color, or weight of the stone that he is using. The limitations of marble may invite no little of the sculptor's pattern. This might be called keeping the medium alive. The director brings the actor's own truth to the creation of the larger truth that the director is after.

If, for example, then, you have, as in Lenormand's *Les Ratés*, a scene in which a crude black man is brought suddenly to the discovery of a corpse and cries aloud, it ought to be true that the first thing to do is to let the actor make the cry himself, express his own kind of emotion in his own kind of cry, and then to use all this as far as possible rather than to start by explaining the emotion and giving him a cry to imitate. If an actor, rehearsing for the storm scene in *King Lear*, feels a certain way in the part, the director may use this feeling as far as he can toward the creation of the feeling that he himself wishes to express. He must believe that his actors are souls as well as bodies, and that the creation he seeks is composed of all our human elements. In sum, such a use of the actor medium by the director ought to be the means of keeping his performance alive in all its parts, as a good painter keeps the paint or a good sculptor keeps the marble alive in every inch of his surface.

DUSE

Duse's last visit to America, called to a sudden stop by her death before the end of the season, brought to our theatre an influence and quality that no words can record. Duse was not primarily and glowingly of the theatre. I should not say that she was the greatest actor that I have seen, but that she seemed of them all the greatest artist. More than any other Duse brought to the art of acting the largest and most poignant idea, the profoundest sensitivity, the deepest and most exquisite response to experience. Of all the people in the theatre she had most that was in common with great poetry, joy, sorrow and beauty, great living. But her acting was, as one saw very quickly, a mere fragment of her. You got the sense in her that her art arose from her life and what she was, as the form of waves and their light and color arise from the large realm of the sea.

You never heard of Duse in such terms as were current about Bernhardt, for example, whose splendors long since dazzled the world of men, and whose art had something about it that was easily detected by the average audience as art.

Bernard Shaw's famous comparison between Duse and Bernhardt has really done very little beyond indicating to sympathetic readers how Duse might affect the emotions of certain of her admirers and how little Shaw could understand in the art of the stage, or of the frankly theatrical art, how far aesthetically from a theatre critic he remained. His two articles and various passages dealing with these two theatre artists have all Shaw's persuasion and witty spell; they are the very essence of the engaging. He has decided to do in, as far as possible, those manifestations of theatre, in this case Bernhardt, that do not accord with what he has decided the theatre should be, as that theatre was exemplified in Ibsen and in Shaw's Superman Wagner, and in— let us not forget, for that is characteristic of Shaw —the plays that Shaw himself was writing or intended to write, praise and champion.

On the side of theatre aesthetics we need only quote a little from *Dramatic Opinions and Essays,* around page 120 for example. The scene in *Gismonda,* a play of the Middle Ages, where a child is "dropped into a tiger's cage as a cue for Madame Bernhardt's popular scream" or when the "inevitable, stale, puerile love scene is turned on to show off that 'voix celeste' which Madame Bernhardt, like a sentimental New England villager with an American organ, keeps always pulled out" . . . "her acting, which is the art of

making you admire her, pity her, champion her,
weep with her, laugh at her jokes, follow her
fortunes breathlessly and applaud her wildly
when the curtain falls. It is the art of finding out
all our weaknesses and practicing on them, cajol-
ing you, harrowing you, exciting you—on the
whole fooling you." Or speaking of Duse, page
136, "The shadows on her face were grey, not
crimson; her lips are sometimes nearly grey also;
there are neither dabs nor dimples; her charm
could never be imitated by a barmaid with un-
limited pin money and a row of footlights instead of the handles of the beer-engine."

Delightful as this may be to read, and has so
often proved to be, this is very silly stuff as
dramatic criticism, and is only middle-class morality at that. What are our weaknesses? What
is weak in us, and gullible therefore for the stage
tricks? What is weakness anyhow? Is it longing
to see splendor, or high heroic patterns instead
of photographs, or glamorous sex, or what?
Should we refuse to accept any make-believe?
Duse told me that she hated Mrs. Alving (Shades
of Shaw if he had been told that!); should she
have presented only that hatred to us?

Finally, to cut short a discussion long since
passée, as it were, the more we understand Bernhardt, her school of the theatre, great and small,
majestic or mediocre or cheap, the more we understand the school that Duse's art exemplified,

sometimes for better, sometimes for worse. In some cases, she said to me, she had to do certain rôles because of her age and her unwillingness to play rôles obviously younger than she was. But it is only in a given realistic theory of theatre art that this argument is theoretically sound. It could be as limited as Bernhardt's limiting the portrayal of her rôles to old women—in that case where would her *Phèdre* be, so universally admired as it was?

In *La Princesse Lointaine* it was all laughable when Bernhardt's champion or a fighting ship arrived; they had better go to Bayreuth and watch the first acts of *Lohengrin* or *Tristan.* Et cetera. But as a matter of fact Duse had some not-too-unabsurd scenes in *Francesca da Rimini.* And the great Chinese actor, Mei Lan Fang, was repelled and astonished by the German singers and their gestures at the Metropolitan.

Bernhardt's genius was essentially public in its character; and there was no wit so slow or so untutored and no eye so dull as not to know that when she played, the universal elements were shaken, and passions that might have been domesticated and blurred by now became suddenly glamorous and superb. That Bernhardt was limited is obvious. She had a limited range of ideas, such ideas, for instance, as amorous seduction, pain and anger—the famous rage through tears —and the infinite throes of dying. She had cer-

tain type conceptions—limited in scope though
not in raw force—of the passionate, the ornate,
the regal, the comic, the poetic. She had vast mo-
notonies of temperament, however brilliant or
strong. Her physical equipment—most of all the
immortal voice—was extraordinary but limited
in possibilities of style. Bernhardt had, too, an
undiluted egotism that very often swamped the
play, the other actors, and everything else save
the audience's response to herself. To her all art
was a passion of self, a splendor of an artist's
mood, though to her, also, art was the only important thing in the world.

The public saw always that Bernhardt was
a stupendous event in human enterprises. She
amazed, thrilled, defeated them; she dominated
even if she taxed them; she delighted, exalted,
and made them shiver with ice on their spines.
She established, apart from herself and the moment of life that she wrought to her stage purposes, a magnificent whole idea, a popular image
that was unforgettable, almost mythical even.
People found in her something they could recognize though they might not be able to moralize
it. They could see in her a kind of sheer life principle which they could enjoy without being able
to understand, something in her that the instinct
of life in them drove them toward as a magnificent example of what they sensed to be the
springs of all our energy and imagination—I

mean elemental power. Duse, of all people, recognized and studied this in Bernhardt. Of that we have the record from her earlier career in the Bologna theatre.

With Duse there was no such thing. She could never have been an overpowering actress in the ordinary sense. She could not even have recited as Bernhardt was able to do, in any elaborate, heroic diction and with any of that incomparable vocal spell that Bernhardt knew how to weave. Artists over Europe were drawn to her almost unendurable tenderness and truth; in Italy her audiences alternately worshipped and railed at her. With her there was nothing audacious and spectacular, nothing violent, seductive, or world-wide. Her glamour was of another sort.

Duse was not the equal mimic in any and all styles, as Garrick seems to have been. She could never have lifted a rôle to any classic fatality and splendor as Mounet Sully could do in *Œdipus*. She had not a certain golden lustre that Ellen Terry had. She could not have exhibited that wild animality, speed, passion and impetus that Mimi Aguglia at her best moments appears to exercise without effort; as Grasso does also, and others of the Sicilian theatre. She had nothing of that romantic epic style that Chaliapin brings to Boris. She had none of the gusto and bravura of an actor like Coquelin. And Réjane had more brilliance.

Some of these qualities and accomplishments Duse obviously might have had if her nature and idea had led her to the classical heroic or the seductive or the highly veneered, the stylized, the violent, the brilliantly comic, or superbly epical. She might have crowned some tradition or school. On the contrary, however, when we come to Duse in the art of acting, it must be said that she was one of those artists, appearing from time to time in every art, who tend to break down the long and painfully built structure of the art they profess. To them their mere craft is only a clutter of old boards, rags, a necessary but obstructing shell. Their passion is truth, an immediate and urging truth in them. These artists by their labor and gifts master the domain of the art with a security and completeness that few artists professing it can ever hope to approach. But whatever craft one of these artists masters he smashes, restates, forces to vanish, scorns save only as a means to an end. Duse could never be a school or a craft, her method was herself. She would have nothing of acting for itself; she was like those who despise their bodies save only as the body disappears before the spirit within that is to be revealed. She had no tricks, no efforts to attract or pique or impress, but only the desire to exist in the life to which she had given herself for those two hours on the stage, only the desire to convey to us and to confirm for herself the infinity of living within the woman she portrayed there. This detachment and intense absorption with the truth that she endured and expressed gave Duse's art its extraordinary purity, its freedom of all exterior considerations and effects.

And so it was that you could not easily get from Duse's acting a pure acting delight. She was not the actor's actor, as Velasquez was the painter's painter, or Spenser the poet's poet. That is to say, you could not delight in her performance as supreme craft, something that delights whether it is deep or flitting, delights because of the perfection of its brush, its tone, its manner, because of its competency, because of its happy application of the art practised, because of the possibilities in it for pleasure in its sheer technical purity and perfection, regardless of everything in life outside it. Something in you withheld you from saying what a beautiful gesture that was, what a tone, what a contrivance in that scene, what reading in this, what technical facility. There was no device to rejoice in, nothing technical to extricate and set aside as a studied piece of skill; there was no eloquence, no recitation, no obvious arrangement or technical economy or evident accomplishment. All these things are good in themselves, of course; they, too, may be almost in themselves a kind of art. They are means of speaking, dialects for ideas; and, after

all, art is art, not life. They lead straight toward
an exhibition of style. Style, however, in the
sense of an added elaboration and distinction of
method, of something in itself creative and separable, style in that separable aspect of facility,
skill or tact, Duse rarely had. And it was
only slowly and almost unwillingly that her art
would allow you an academic enjoyment; it
would not yield itself to the mere choice judgments of a sophistication in taste. Duse would
not grant you that kind of appreciation. It was
as if she would accept no love but the love for
all herself and the cost that followed.

Only slowly did you see what labor and skill
had gone to make up that creation of Duse's
soul in the outer forms of an art. In *Così Sia*
you saw her bending over the child, you saw
her carry the pilgrim's staff, the lines of her long
garments, the pity of her hands, the wandering
of her hands among the lights on the altar. You
saw suddenly that dumbness and then that flut-
ter of life through the body. You saw that the
entire moment had revealed itself to you. You
saw what this woman knew; and you wondered
whether such a knowledge of the human life and
soul resolved itself in her finally into tears or into
light. But it was only gradually that you were
aware of how Duse suggested perpetually a state
of music which must have come from a long love
and study of that art; and of how this quality

was in evidence always, in her visual aspect, in the tone, and in her total conception of the part. And slowly you perceived Duse's years of familiarity with the lines of statuary, and the extent to which she had mastered from great sculpture the inevitable lines of grace and meaning, and had learned from it how to study the rhythms of the form she sought and to free these rhythms of all but that last beauty of its own characteristics.

People were numerous who objected to Duse's gestures, the rhythm of her hands, her perpetual use of draperies and arrangements of pose. To make this objection is to confuse her art with what we ordinarily recognize and require as realism. To insist on her giving up these gestures and these flowing lines is to take away one of her mediums of expression. It would be to sacrifice for mere imitative probability the possibilities of another language. Duse could find an outer image that seemed to be wholly the inner thought that she expressed. This visual statement was not a copy of something which we may see in life and from which we may guess the inner thought; no, it exhibited—as great painting does or great sculpture—a visual design as free of or as faithful to actual nature as the artist chooses to make it. To appreciate Duse's rhythms of garments and bodily movements you needed to be able to do more than recognize mere fidelity to natural human life and its ways, you had to understand the visual medium itself, to be able to see and read it, precisely as you understand music by being able to hear it and not by recognizing its resemblance to familiar sounds, to birds, bells, or stormy weather. Duse could not be understood unless one knew that these gestures and these lines were in themselves a great art; that they were added to her other mediums of expression as melody is added to the mere meaning of words.

Duse knew how to keep the mass and the line alive. She knew, like a great painter or sculptor, what degree of mere description, imitation, re-production to put into an action, a posture, a gesture that is taken from nature; and at the same time she could give her line a life of its own, a meaning that was eventually independent of the thing she interpreted. She knew from the visual arts that no movement of gesture or line arises suddenly of itself, but that it must always exist as a part of a whole, must achieve its aptness and beauty not out of its limited, sudden self, but out of a mass of relationships; in sum, she knew what few actors know at all, that a line or gesture must begin and end. Duse knew subtly and inexplica-bly how to give to her very presence, to her body, as she was present on the stage, a radiance and a difference, like a creation in art. Her figure there remained in the mind as something at the same time both luminous and abstract.

And finally there was a quality in Duse's art of which sometimes you were aware as you watched her playing, and sometimes unaware until days afterward, when the sense of it grew and filled your thoughts. This quality in what she did was the presence of mind. Not mind in the shape of a problem, an intellectual if rather obvious analysis or thesis, but a pervading thing far more profound.

You may take, for an example, the first act of Ibsen's *Ghosts;* what Duse did in it was a technical and spiritual marvel. The first act of *Ghosts* as Ibsen wrote it has an undercurrent of fine dramatic power and a sharp edge of truth. But in the course of the writing a provincialism and drabness of conception more than once appears; Mrs. Alving and her author are now and again insistent and parochial, and without either taste or imagination. Ibsen's Mrs. Alving falls into platitude, stubborn and firm. Duse turned such passages into what is not platitude, but passionate memory. What in Ibsen's lines is only half placed culturally—his reflections on life, his debates, analyses—Duse established easily in right relation to a wide culture and distinction. Meantime she set forth the idea that should dominate the play as she saw it: the idea of maternal love and of a being whose body and whose love are interposed between her son and universal law.

Ibsen's drama of *The Lady from the Sea* has

turns of psychology, biology, romance, symbolic poetry, and homely comedy, beginning stalely, running into a region with deep fascination to it, and winding up in a muddle of pseudo-scientific and moralistic explanations, manias, obsessions, freedom of choice, responsibility, and the like. It is outmoded now, but much of it was always without imagination or unifying power. What Duse did with *The Lady from the Sea* was like what she had done with many another play, with Galeratti-Scotti's *Così Sia,* for example, in which she took the simple story of a mother who had sacrificed all for her son only to be deserted by him, and gave to it her own marvellous conception of the nature of love. It was maternal love, to be sure, that Duse expressed; but this, after all, may be the greatest love theme, since it comprises all love; it is a love that begins with the desire to create out of its own body the body of a child, and then to go on forever creating its own mind and soul in the child's soul and the child's mind. Such love underlies all life and expresses the process of all nature, which proceeds from physical substance to idea, and which within its mortal bodies creates its immortal forms and qualities.

When Ibsen's Ellida comes on the stage, with her restlessness, her hunger for the sea, her sense of the Stranger's power drawing her, we get some touch of mystery, no doubt, but also a strong suggestion of explanation; a diagnosis is suggested; the woman is neurotic, suffering from an obsession. When Duse's Ellida came on the scene what we got was a poetic idea, a thing free and complete in our minds, caught there like a light in the momentary shell of a human body. The woman was literally neurotic, yes, if you like, sick with a state of mind, exactly as we might say that she was a man's wife or breathed with her lungs. But that had little to do with the point, which consisted in the wonder of this thing felt, the singleness and purity of this mood, this dream of freedom, this affinity that affrights and allures. For this the woman there on the stage is the vessel. It is this that is permanent and beautiful and that drives forever toward the immortal; it is this that is both poetic and—and here with Duse science found its right place—that is both poetic and biological. The truth Duse discovers thus, has that oneness of life at its heights and depths that art only at its best moments can achieve.

Ibsen's play came to its final idea. The Stranger reappears. Ellida is free to choose. What Duse creates then concerns love and freedom. A complete and limitless love, she tells us, is as vast as the sea and as infinite, and is itself the ultimate human freedom. The body of Wangel stands between Ellida and the body of the Stranger who has come to take her away; the love defeats the power that has haunted and destroyed her soul. And because this love is boundless and wide and inexhaustible, it, even more than the sea, allures and affrights her and feeds and consumes her life. This love, even more than the sea, can become her mystery.

With that conception and illumination that Duse brought to the theme of Ibsen's drama the whole is lifted into poetry. She did to it what would have happened at the hands of a great poet. She threw light upon it, dilated it, discovered in it what is most significant and essential, and gave to that an existence of its own, a complete life. She discovered for it the right relation of the concrete to the ideal, of the phenomenon, the accident, to the permanent, the essential. And she created for this idea a form inseparable from it.

If Duse could dilate thus an Ibsen conception and give to it its due place in a larger cosmos of feeling and idea, her impress on the works of slighter dramatists would plainly go yet farther; it served either to remake or destroy them. To her a drama or a character exhibited only some power of life that lay in it; and so to hollow rôles, like many of Sardou's and of the ordinary theatre, she brought a devastating light; she acted out of herself some beauty and meaning that the dramatist had never imagined; and what he had not felt, of love, irony, radiance, she felt and created in the rôle.

You needed to see Duse in a shallow rôle like Sudermann's Magda or as Camille, or to watch her through a scene like that last of *The Lady from the Sea,* and then, when it was over, review and sum up what she had accomplished, if you would realize her quality. You saw then more and more that such a gradation of emphasis throughout a play, and so fine and so elusive but unforgettable a comprehension of the entire meaning of the character and theme could come only from a remarkable ability and an association with culture and ideas, combined with a poetic and reflective nature, with a grace of spirit, with a courage of mind, and, finally, with something throughout the personality, quiet and taken for granted, I mean that kind of untouched and unstressed and constant spiritual audacity that moves great natures.

Duse not only illustrated the quality of the poetic as it applies not to poetry alone but to every other art. She illustrated the nature of realism in general, especially of that best Italian realism, which is so capable of rendering by means of only actual or possible external details the inmost idea. To speak of Duse's as stark realism, as was sometimes done, makes no sense. If you observed her well you saw that she never

represented or reproduced or counterfeited anything. Actions the most literal were yet removed
from the actual; everything that Duse did had
a certain removal and restatement to it. Every
action she presented borrowed light from her.

When you know well the Greek marbles in
the Naples Museum, you realize how subtly individual they are; types, yes, but within the security of the type intensely varied and singly
felt. But in the north you meet with the sculpture of the younger Renaissance. You see not
the type become real and individual, not, as in
the classic, the poetry of the individual soul set
forth with reticent intensity in universal forms.
What you see is the individual reality, the very
surface of the thing portrayed, set down with
such spiritual and physical precision that its soul
becomes its body and its body its soul. In the
work of Desiderio da Settignano, Mino da Fiesole, Benedetto da Maiano and others you perceive a singular distinction in fidelity combined
with ideal feeling. The portrait of the bishop at
Fiesole, how much the man it is, but how removed from him and brought into our souls by
the artist's taste and imperceptible style! The
Guidarello Guidarelli at Ravenna, a little too direct, in the face at least too close to a mere likeness, but how full of intensity of life and animation, how full of death, too, how simply tragic
and yet how subtle and elaborate in its surface

planes and its comment on the young spirit within! Mino da Fiesole adds to Holbein, for example, a singular sweetness, relaxation, and grace of culture. He has an ease and poetry of distinction where Holbein has distinction of artistic conscience and character. And Rosellino's tomb for the young cardinal at Samminiato, those fine and sensitive nostrils, those still, perfect hands quieted in death, the mouth droll and clear, almost alive and yet remote with death, the modelling under the chin sagging slightly down with its own weight and yet suggesting the idea of weight rather than the sagged flesh and mere accident of it, the closed eyes and the shadows under them, the still breast with the breath now taken somehow out of it—what exact and literal truth in all this, and yet what invisible style and what distinguished approach to the actual detail, what learning and culture and reflection! And underneath all this and putting the life into it, what an endowment of sheer animal talent and vitality! This, then, can be realism; though not the realism that we have heard so much about in France, where Zola and his school have reigned and where Henri Becque and Flaubert have written their gray masterpieces; not the realism of Dutch painting, with its grotesque or brutal detail or its sound honesty, as the case might be; and not the gracious and ample realism of Velasquez. Like Dante's, though less poetic, less concrete, less intense, the realism of this sculpture is. And this was Duse's realism. It is a comment on the fact that Duse, though she was in long revolt against schools and classic formularies and almost against her craft itself, had yet no violence, no excess, and no accidents, because she kept her art close to her spirit and made sure that it expressed herself.

The poetic and realistic in Duse is further commented upon by her relation to D'Annunzio's art. D'Annunzio's gift is untranslatable into English; it is a gift for expression almost abnormal, a sensitivity to the color of experience carried beyond bounds, an abandonment to life, sensations and ideas that is in itself a kind of power. Together with these faculties D'Annunzio has a gift for style, for words. He achieves an orchestration of whatever single line he chooses to follow. It is easy to see why, and not solely for personal reasons, as people like to think, Duse followed his art and in the face of obstacles forced on the public his plays, though she knew well their dramatic defects. Her art had none of D'Annunzio's recurrent falsity or specious images. It was more ordered than his, more in scale, more wisely and sweetly seen, more sorrowfully human, more universal in meaning and appeal. But D'Annunzio's plays brought to the service of drama the poetic mind, which she not only valued as a more luminous element than some basic social philosophy or superior craft in the theatre, but knew also to be far less often found there. D'Annunzio's plays gave her a constant, beautiful release of the life in her; they poured her spirit out on things, on people, on thought; they created her over and over and lighted her genius with the genius of another.

When she talked with you Duse used to come straight across the room and sit near, her fingers sometimes touching your arm. She spoke fluently and beautifully in varied images like those of poetry and with clearly made points. She spoke of herself, her art, of you, your ideas and work, but always with a kind of deep egotism that seemed both personal and impersonal. It seemed an egotism without humor, but above the need for it, non-social but divinely human and true. It bore interestingly on her relation to artists; every one knows that the artists were numberless who drew from Duse inspiration, encouragement, fecundation of their talents; through them she became long before her death a great pathetic myth. Duse obliterated and exalted you. There was something about her central intensity that was like the creative impulse itself, like sexual love, and like creation in an artist. It was penetrating and oblivious at the same time. It ignored and held you. She reduced

you to nothing and gave you at the same moment the sense of being taken as no mere individual but as something in yourself that was immortal. You felt ashamed to think of yourself or
of the disconcerting oversight of your presence;
and yet at the same moment you felt concerned
only with what might be your eternal self. She
gave you an unescapable, cruel life. You felt
that after her there was no peace any more, not
ever, but—in so far as you were alive at all—
only the pressure and necessity and travail of
creation, *la mia delizia ed erinni,* as Leonardo
said of art, the delight and torment. And yet
you felt the kindest humanity and affection and
interest, you brought your life of small affairs
to her as to a gentle, wise mother.

It is interesting that Duse's face, wonderful
as it was, was even more wonderful on the stage
than when seen near to. Duse had a mask that
was theatrical in the highest sense. The proportions of her face had a character that or-
ganized into something even finer under the
visual conditions of the stage, under the *optique
du théâtre.* The space between the eyes; the definite upper lips above the dark eyes; the length
of the upper lip; the proportions of the cheek-
bones and the brow; the ample mouth and distinct teeth, with the modelling of the chin; were
all such as the light, distance, and interrelation-
ships of the theatrical scene could bring to great

expressiveness and beauty. The same was true of her voice, which gained in beauty and expressiveness when brought to the pitch and rhythm of the stage. Duse's face, seen close, was not so tragic as it looked on the stage, because of the play of interest that you could see upon it. But the immense sadness of this face came partly from the mere physical conformation, which in its sheer design was pathetic. There was also the record of pain and illness and of unfortunate or consuming events in her own experience. But over and above all these, and giving the final tragic heightening to Duse's face, was something that derived, I think, from the fact that her suffering arose most from the collision of her idealism with the mere ordinary conditions of life. From her living, her thought, and her emotion, she evolved her conceptions and ideas; and she saw these constantly defeated by the incompleteness and death in things.

Duse gave you first the impression of a certain strength, which came from the clear rhythms of her physical presence and from the ardor of her spirit when she talked. But she seemed frail too, partly from exhaustion and partly from a terrible sensitivity. Always after seeing her the thought came to you of what people from her audiences have so often mentioned, I mean the feeling she aroused of defense, the impulse to protect her. This impulse when you were face to face with her, hearing her talk, you seemed to feel less. She seemed to possess strength for her own ends and a profound vitality. But afterward, the moment you left, there grew in your thoughts a marvellous poignancy, and with it this defense of her. This, I think, arose from your feeling of the intense presence in her of that element that we know is life, fragile, poignant, necessary.

Looking at her you thought of the question, so often debated, of Duse's neglect of the advantages of make-up on the stage; and it seemed probable that she avoided elaborate make-up not only in order, as we have heard so long, to let the living written on her face be read for its own truth, not only for this reason but also because she had found that, save for a little underscoring, her mask was both too fluid and too marked to do anything but lose under paint and paste.

Duse in her last season, now past sixty, when the poverty following the war and perhaps a desire to express her art for the younger theatre had sent her back to the stage, did not suggest age so much as she suggested a diminished endurance; it was a question more of quality than quantity. That is to say, you could see clearly that the actress might not be able to go on for so long or so many performances, or for violent scenes, but it was also equally clear that for what she did her body lacked nothing and was adequate in the most exact meaning of the word. Duse kept her old physical co-ordination; the flow of lines was still perfect and continuous; there was no sense of stiffness or angularity, or, as nearly always happens with age, of that lessening in the power of the muscles to carry out the will. The voice was less clear and vibrant than once, but no less dramatic and penetrating. There was still to be heard that constant surprise and strange, quiet vitality in rhythm which she employed in her reading, and by which she gave, very often without using any other means, so terrible a sense of life. Looking at Duse's figure there on the stage you got pretty much what you always got, the sense of a body that had no existence apart from its idea. As had always been so, her art connected with her presence as music is connected with sound.

And in one respect above all Duse triumphed. She made no attempt to reproduce what as a younger artist she had once done. It was no revival of former creations, no cheating of time and our memories that she gave. She did not strain after looking young, or paint and plaster herself into a pretty dolly, but played throughout in her own terms; she restated her dramatic material in terms of the Duse that she was at the present time, not only in appearance, but also—what is much more subtle and difficult—

spiritually and mentally. In this achievement, and in the intention behind it, was illustrated, as much as in any fact about her, the nature of Duse's art and of her mind.

The same thing, I have thought, that made Duse's art illustrate the nature of all arts, made her in herself not only representative of our universal life, which is the soul, but also intensely representative in her own kind. She was, after all, profoundly Italian and profoundly feminine. She had about her something of the Italian country. That land brought by so much labor and devotion, and through so many years of work and living, to such beauty and civilization, seems after all most easy and natural and gently taken for granted. Its air and color and light, though they may be either meadows and green valleys thick with almond and olive trees, or volcanic fierce regions, harsh and touched with death, have, every day when the right hours fall, a divine sweetness come over them, often something elegiac, something that is ancient, poignant, and grave. And those towns over Italy, after long centuries of art and living, present every one of them something that is its own, and that seems to simplify all that went to make it up into at last a vivid and uninsistent whole, with its own character and truth. And everywhere in Italy the famous *combinazione* is to be seen, the faculty of taking whatever one wills out of any style or age or origin, and putting it where one pleases and adding to it whatever one likes to have added. Freedom and naturalness of choice and absence of the academic are almost the first quality in the aspect of Italian towns. And this labor, apparent ease, unity, freedom were the first quality in the aspect of Duse's art, which drew from many regions but lived always in one, and which used its culture for ends so immediate and necessary that it could not be pedantic or highly schooled.

The sweetness and harmony and poignant precision that Duse had were Italian, and a certain tragic literalness and warmth of mind. She had the Italian consuming life, with its simplicity and directness of approach combined with what is subtle and highly complex. In the deepest sense Duse seemed the most feminine of all artists. It was not so much in the traits usually spoken of, now satirically, now sentimentally, as characteristic of women, it was rather something in a last fundamental quality by which women may differ from men. There was supremely in her that virginal or pure quality that women have when they love or give themselves as instruments by which, through the birth of a child, life is created anew. There was in Duse this quintessence of the woman, a divine generosity, a purity of response, a beautiful singleness of mood, an absorption with living values without other considerations, an existence universal and personal rather than social, a body and soul that are solitary and infinite with the principle of generation, a fatalism and pity that come from a nearness to birth and death.

You constantly heard and read of Duse's sadness, of the tragic element that was said to be always present in her, and that was admired or resented by the spectators as the case might be. But whether you were either depressed or left impatient, or bound forever by this, it is more profitable to think of such a quality in Duse and her art as deriving not so much from sadness as from a certain impression of finality. In her art the thing presented, the action, the thought, took on the pathos of finality, something of the far, perfect line, the hail and farewell. There was in it for us somehow a nostalgia, a tragic sense of beauty and completion.

To people for whom Duse's art was a power and a new impulse of life, her supreme quality was what lay behind no art in particular, but behind all art: the response to life. The poet, the musician, the painter and architect, and actor or dancer, and the saint, also, whose life and ways possess the continuity and creative passion of art, all draw life to them by their capacity for it. In them life is gathered, it refracts, simplifies, finds out its essential and eternal principle or idea and a new body for it, and so goes on. And in Duse of all artists people most felt the thing they most respond to in all living: an infinity of tragic wonder and tenderness.

TWO THEATRES

IF YOU go to the People's Theatre and then to the Royal, a block away on the Bowery, you will discover a happy kinship in the world of men and art. The Yiddish actors are at one theatre, the Sicilian at the other; and at both places the actor and audience are children of the Mediterranean. The Jews draw farther back in time from Asia Minor; the South Italians have blood in them from the Greeks and Romans, the Africans, Saracens, Normans, Spanish, French, and the first island tribes, whoever they were; and are as little like Florentines to-day as they are like the Danes or the Belgians. Both of these are folk theatres, and for that reason the elements to be observed in them are perhaps more fundamental; and the two of them together supply one of those cases of repetition and variation within our microcosm that can teach us so much about art.

There is no actor at the Jewish theatre, of course, to compare with Grasso; though among its company I have seen Miss Gersten exhibit a power and a terrible sincerity hardly surpassed in all New York. But in both these theatres there is the same atmosphere of animation, intense interest, response. In both the same tide flows between actors and audiences; both audiences give themselves to the play; the plays at both are melodramas and the story is the thing; there is the same hum of comment and easy judging, like wonderful children together. Among the actors there is the same vividness, the same expressiveness of eyes and hands and shoulders. And you get the same sense of tremendous and inexhaustible vitality on the stage and in the house, the capacity for strong food, strong bodies, strong emotions and crises of living.

Then presently in the midst of the similarity the differences begin to appear.

These people of the Jewish theatre are a race apart in every country they dwell in. They cling to their own culture. In New York there are eleven Jewish theatres and two vaudeville houses. But the Italians, in so far as they are mindful of it at all, have not bothered very much about their racial culture. They have brought along bits of it with them as they have brought certain vegetables, finocchi, scarola, and zucchini. But as for their culture it is safe at home; it has its own land, and they, in this year 1923, have still no permanent theatre in New York.

The Jews in this People's Theatre have come here from lands more northern than the cradle of their race, and their ancient habit of living

has been driven even farther inward. Their audiences like to enter seriously into the conscience of a play; they like the story romantic,
of love and virtue triumphant, the villain blackly
damned. The Sicilians take more simply the surface of life. Their plays have a way of progress-
ing through every-day prose, joy, dancing, love,
battle, murder, and sudden death without any
particular comment or moral winding up. *The
God of Mercy*, after long labor of twilights,
wrongs, rough comedy, and ruined homes, ends
with a farm scene, hay, milk, the hills, the child,
and triple innings for the villain. In *The Wolf*
there is a festa and flowers; the mother is in love
with the daughter's husband, who drives her out
with an axe; her cry is heard, and the murderer
rushes through with the horror of his crime on
every inch of him; and there the curtain drops;
though, as everybody knows, the carabinieri will
get him and take him to prison, unless, that is,
he has already run off to the bandits. All of
which sounds simple and might be childish but
for Grasso's magnificent art, an art so right, so
inevitable and complete that nothing empty that
it touches can remain so and nothing real elude
a greater reality. No Jewish art could take all
that so directly. The elements of our life, its
feeling, impulses, crises, are taken by these Sicilians as the elements of nature are taken; as
the lightning that scorches, moonlight and peace,

the sun, night, darkness. These forces are in this
Sicilian art what they were with the Greeks;
the life of man in these plays strikes against passion, rage, revenge, hunger, and death, as nature encounters wind and sun and drouth and
the verdure of the rain.

The Yiddish acting is more complex, and in
that sense, at least, more modern. It has the realism of intense feeling, and a deep respect for
that feeling. Its best effects come from a compulsive rendering of that intensity, and whatever beauty there may be is a spiritual beauty,
almost without appeal to the eye. In its best
moments it sacrifices everything to this spiritual
truth, and beyond that its interest in beauty
seems comparatively slight, whether beauty of
manner, style, or appearance. But the Sicilian
art is more beautiful to the eye, with more grace,
more flowing and flexible lines, more bright-
ness and color in the voice and gestures, more
abundance, as that lovely country has from which
it comes. Compared to the Sicilian this Jewish
art has infinities of mood; it has, too, more biting
pain, more sentiment; and it has a deep tenderness where the Sicilian has only the tenderness of simple affection or erotic impulse,
nothing poignant, searching, understanding or
profound. When we come to the other side of
the picture, to the defect of this excellence, we
find that the Yiddish art on its poorer side sinks

into sentimentality, the mawkish, theatrical, insincere, tricky, and false. And it is often at the same time vulgar. On its poorest side the Sicilian acting becomes wild and childish, mere sensation and event and explosion. But it is rarely sentimental, though it is often passionate. It makes violent appeals sometimes but few cheap ones. And it is never vulgar, though it is brutal enough. It has the animality and refinement of nature itself. The Sicilian realism is open; it is easily copied after the current of life. In this sense it is supremely natural, the most natural in any theatre. Its best effects are this naturalness in the display of terrific passions.

This passionate art of the Sicilians exercises us without depressing us; we may shed tears but we are not glum about it. It may leave us with something of Aristotle's katharsis, a purging that comes from bringing us so vividly into play. Or it may leave us excited, flushed, exhausted, as wild beasts in a cage can do. But it does not leave us in a mood. We may grieve over what has happened in the scene; but it will not seethe and ferment and revolt in our souls, and we are no more responsible for it socially than we are for an earthquake. We are stirred and shaken and aired by it as we are by the manifestations of nature.

There is, too, about such an art as the Sicilians' a certain harsh indifference that is like the natural world. And it is this, I think, that gives it so strong a hold on the spectator, the sense of those bodies whose magnetism draws to themselves the forces of man's life, and whose eloquence conveys to us man's passion and fatality. At its best this Sicilian art has the beauty and ferocity and pathos of human life seen strictly as one with the earth.

THE FLOWER

THE stand that the Nō Plays take on the place of actuality in the theatre is shown best by their ghosts. In play after play, out of the several hundred that the Japanese possess, and in almost every Nō translated by Fenollosa, Waley, and others, the leading character of the piece is a ghost, is not the hero or the heroine about whose life and deeds the play is made, but an apparition.

Seami, who was born in 1363 and who with his father stands at the head of the Nō, taught his pupils that in imitation there should always be a tinge of the unlike. And to his mind the reason for this is that if we press imitation too far, it will impinge on reality and will cease to give an impression of likeness. If one aims at only the beautiful, the flower, as he calls it, will be sure to appear. If, for example, in the part of an old man the actor, merely because he has noticed that old men walk with bent backs and crooked knees and have shrunken frames, sets about to imitate these characteristics, he may indeed achieve an effect of decrepitude, but it will be at the expense of the flower. And if the flower be lacking there will be no beauty in the impersonation. What this actor should study, Seami says, is that effect of will without the corresponding capacity for action that shows in old age, and this effect will often be given best by making all movements a little late, so that they come after the musical beat. For in old age the limbs are heavy and the ears slow; there is the will to move but not the corresponding capacity. With this in mind the actor · may then be as lively as he pleases. For an example of this search for the flower and not for the exact imitation in a play, take the *Miidera*. The mother, crazed by the loss of her little boy who has strayed away, is drawn by the sound of the bell over the lake and valley to its temple, where she finds the priests in the garden gazing at the autumn moon, the little boy among them. She is at length allowed to toll the bell herself, and she and her little son recognize each other. In this play everything turns on the sound of the bell, its power over the heart, its memory, its gentleness. But in the presentation, since so much depends upon just that sound, there is no attempt to represent the bell, only the movement of tolling it is given.

All this is summed up in the ghosts. It is better, the Nō artists believe, to have the hero come again to this life, drawn by some depth of desire in him or in some one in the living world below; for in this way reality is avoided, the outward form is that of a ghost but within is the heart of a man, and out of this heart the actors can draw for the matter of their art those dreams and passions, that sorrow and pride and fate, whose poignant energy was the life of the hero's body when he lived and after death the life of his soul. Freed in this way of the actual reality, the artist works only through the imagination as he chooses, aiming only at the beautiful.

In the performance of the Nōs, in their development, and in the rôles, we can find an indispensable commentary on Greek drama. The Nōs carry us farther than anything else in the theatre of the world toward a clear conception of the Greek; they carry our insight farther yet into the Greek dramatic form, into its ritualistic nature, its use of the chorus, and the method by which its more or less fixed outline is filled in and developed by means of lyrical details. And most of all they illuminate the heroic character of the Greek rôles—to take the heroic strictly in the classical sense of the sublimation of the instincts of the multitude in one heroic breast.

The Nōs begin with the entrance of the assistant, the *waki*, the second character, who names himself, his origin, his destination at the moment. Then comes the Song of Travel, faintly drawn like an old painting on silk, to quicken the imagination so that we may travel with the speaker and be ready at last for the heroic entry. Then comes the *shite,* the central character, or rather the ghost of him, and tells his story. There the first part of the drama closes. In the second part the hero lives through again his great moment, the climax of his glory or sorrow or last struggle. The chorus, which has been assisting the leading actor when the words interfered with his dance movements, chants a song then that will give us some poem that emerges from the story; and the hero fades from the stage.

The subjects for the Nō are widely diverse. There is the *Atsumori,* in which the ghost of the young hero tells of his last fight, how he turned back his horse knee-deep in the lashing waves and struck at his enemy, and how afterward they found him lying on the shore, beside him his bamboo flute wrapped in brocade. Or there is the play about Tsunemasa, Atsumori's brother, who had died at the same battle, to whom the Emperor had given a lute called the Green Hill. And now Gyōkei the priest is taking the lute by his master's orders to dedicate it to Buddha, performing then a liturgy of flutes and strings for the salvation of Tsunemasa's soul. In the flame of the candle burning low in the almost spent night the musicians see a shadow dimly appearing, like haze over the fields, they say; it is the ghost of Tsunemasa drawn back to the world by the sound of the strings. And though they cannot see him do it in the faint light, they feel him pluck the lute strings and hear the sound of rain beating on trees and grass. In the *Kagekiyo* there is the exquisite motive where the unhappy girl, whose sleeve is like a flower wet with rain, and who has come to seek her father, once a hero, now a filthy outcast, to ease his shame asks him to recite the story of his great deeds at Yashima. There is the plot of the *Nachi No Ki,* where the hero fallen to poverty cuts down the sole treasures left to him, his three dwarf trees, the pine, cherry, and plum, to warm a traveller, who turns out later to be the Emperor. Or there is the terrific story of Komachi, once a court beauty, but scornful of her lovers, and now wandering, cursed, old, foul, mad. Or the Hoka priests who avenge their father's murder. And there are plays turning on the lives of children, happy some of them, others bitter and sad. But whatever the subject they are seen in a vision, the Nōs, seen always poetically. They illustrate continuously the process by which the poetic mind expresses one part of the world in terms of another; establishes the one thing in terms of the whole; catches the whole in some one happy instance; and thus reveals that kind of radiance of all things among themselves which poetry is.

But it is by all odds the security of their essen-

tial character that makes these plays most interesting. Nine out of every ten of them, however good or bad otherwise, maintain this essential character of dramatic design. They evince
a remarkable proportionment of words, movement, scenic stage details, an emphasis and a
pattern of their own; and through all this they
attain to a singular freedom. Through this they
are apart from all immediacy. Through this they
are enabled not to depend on any direct attack
on our emotions but rather to avoid it—"in
plays," Seami says, in his book on the Nō, "where
a lost child is found by its parents the writer
should not introduce a scene where they clutch
and cling to one another, sobbing and weeping
. . . plays in which children occur, even if well
done, are always apt to make the audience ex-
claim in disgust: 'Don't harrow our feelings in
this way.'" Through this security of an essential character of their own, these plays are as independent as a print of Hokusai's. All reality of
men and actions and material objects is made
to become theirs before these plays can use
them. To suffer translation into their own terms,
men and actions and objective realities, inns,
palaces, temples, waysides, thrones, are turned
into dreams, and dreams into reality; the human
face in characters where a due degree of emotion will be passed, is hidden under the motionless and subtle incantation of the mask; and even

the identity of the actor hero himself is translated into the convention of the chorus, who take his words from him and speak them for him when the fit moment comes. And whether we think them great works or not, we should have to be very ignorant of the fundamentals of dramatic art not to see the singularity and integrity of these plays so securely achieved that they need no heavier device than the dropping of the flute note at the end of a phrase, which always before went up, not down, to show that the scene is ended. And finally, to leave aside the dramatic essence and the rest of it, there is something in the general, all-round quality of these old pieces that is itself like a flute note, and that is like the oldest painting of China, from whose poetry in fact the poetry of the Nō derives: a kind of strange, high, meagre delicacy and fortitude of the heart.

TRANSLATIONS

COMBINATIONS of operas are usually hit-and-miss affairs; but when Mr. John Alden Carpenter's *The Birthday of the Infanta*, with the *décor* by Mr. Robert Edmond Jones, was given after *I Pagliacci*, with the traditional setting, the contrast was luminous. Following the Sicilian story with its hot loves and fierce dramatic lyricism, its tawny and blue and crimson world, and its tawdry and mediocre scene, *The Birthday of the Infanta* brought a strangely different atmosphere. In all of it there was no sex, no glare. Against the passion, laughter, revenge, and death of those strolling players it set up the thin and innocent life of a little Princess of twelve and her court in the midst of the rich, hard magnificence of the circumstance about them. We see first the garden courtyard of the palace. On either hand the high walls rise, flat spaces with long heavy mouldings, gray varied to darker and more ashen tones. To the left at the head of a flight of steps a door, very high, with an inspired touch of grayish white in the baroque metal awning across the curve of the top; and dark red curtains showing through the

glass at the sides. Across the middle of the scene
and between the two walls, a sort of raised terrace and balustrade connecting them, and to
the back a high iron screen through which appear the Spanish mountains, a violet silhouette
hardening to blue against the cold gray-rose of
the sky. It is all grave and austere and cruel and
lovely, elegant, rich, and superb, this place where
the child Princess and her court will make their
festival. And the music meanwhile in that open-
ing moment is austere, a little thin, it is innocent, lonely, continuous; and now and then it
hints at the grotesque and the poignant and the
frail tragedy to come.

The Infanta enters through the great door;
her court surrounds her. They bring in gifts; a
chest with a gown, brocade banded with gal-
loons of gold; a huge silver cage with strange
birds; a painted casket with a doll in a green
farthingale. There is a birthday cake with
lighted candles, there are mock rope-walkers,
jugglers, and a mock bull-fight, when the ladies
have taken their places on the terrace to see.
And then last they bring in the grotesque. He is
Pedro the dwarf and hunchback. He looks
strangely about him, crooks his head, and begins to dance about for the court. He is perplexed, a lonely, vague, ashen little figure amus-
ing the fine company, and clinging to the balustrade as he reaches out his hand to the Princess

above him. The Infanta and her court withdraw. And as the scene ends Pedro eludes his guard, gets his crooked legs through the door just in time, shuts it in the guard's face, and escapes into the palace.

The curtain rises then on the palace vestibule, lofty, with a high door looking out on the same cold-rose sky as before, across a terrace promenade. The scene there in the palace is crimson and gray, dull rose, gold, black. Candlesticks with their huge candles stand ten feet high, and there are two mirrors higher still. The grotesque enters; he is awestruck by the splendor around him, and then he sees the mirrors. Then, as in Oscar Wilde's story, he sees himself for the first time in all his ugliness and deformity; and dances a frenzied dance until he falls dead. After a little the Princess comes in, touches him and calls him to dance for her. But he does not waken, and she sees that he is dead. She lays her red rose on his cheek. They draw her away as the merrymakers from without appear in the door.

All this innocent and grotesque, sombre, ornate gaiety Mr. Carpenter expressed, so austere is his music at times, so macabre, so hauntingly elaborated, so wistful, and so finely withdrawn. This music of the *Infanta* has none of the fury of sex in it, for the lives that it reveals have an ironical innocence and formality; but in them and in their music as well there is the shadow of what will mature into passion. The imagination of the music constantly appears; it sustains a modern quality throughout; it has the excitement of poetic sincerity, and it carries the whole piece toward something that is unescapably drama.

Mr. Robert Edmond Jones's contribution to *The Birthday of the Infanta* if not more significant than his *Macbeth* was more complete. It was the most distinguished thing that he has done so far, it seems to me. And it is, moreover, a fine case to take as an illustration of a point that is clear to very few people and that concerns the art of the theatre as an art strictly to itself. This—to be repeated over and over again —the art of the theatre is not a mere combination of any particular things, setting, actors, recitation, literature, for example; it is a distinct and separate art. It may be composed of many things, but it is none of them. Nothing that goes to compose this art remains as it was before becoming a part of it. The actions represented by the actors are no longer life but action out of life restated in terms of the mood of the play, the dramatic moment, the scene, the characters present. Buildings are no longer architecture, but architecture seen in these new terms. Drama is not literature, but literature in terms of the theatre. The art of the theatre has ultimately its essential character, and differs from painting, literature, architecture, and all its contributory arts as they differ from one another in the essential character that sustains and perpetuates each one of them. For every art justifies its existence by the fact that it expresses what nothing else could express. The difference between a thing said in one art and said in another implies the fundamental difference in the two arts, and this difference of theirs measures their inability to express exactly the same thing. But what that separate art of the theatre is, can be more easily illustrated than defined. As an illustration of it, then, in one single respect out of the many involved, take the setting for the *Infanta*.

Nowhere in Spain have I seen buildings like these. But I have seen in Spain that character of sterility, of color and mass. I have seen that barbaric and cruel barrenness of sheer walls emerge, though any amount of rococo and baroque or plateresque ornamentation had been superficially laid on to soften the aspect of it. And I have seen in Spain this cold elegance pushed to the romantic; as in the Escorial, where Philip's simplicity becomes at length a glowing and sinister affectation. The character of Mr. Jones' settings, then, perfectly express the Spanish instinct which all over Spain we see translated by her architectural artists into the actuality of buildings. But that is not the important point just here. So far these settings of Mr. Jones' may have become architectural art, it is true, but they are not necessarily the art of the theatre. The important thing to be said here is that this is not architecture but a translation of architecture into theatre terms.

The same is true in a region even more difficult perhaps, and certainly more elusive, the costumes. These costumes in the *Infanta* were not particularly interesting as reproductions of Spanish fashions toward the end of the seventeenth century. I have seen much better copies than they were or tried to be. And they were not mere clothes such as we used to see in a careful Clyde Fitch production, or garments that were costly enough and exactly borrowed from history, as in Miss Doris Keane's *Czarina*, or as Mansfield used to have with his famous copies of Beau Brummel's buttons and jewelry. None of these things. These costumes for the *Infanta* were distinguished because they were Spanish seventeenth-century costumes seen superbly in terms of the theatre. They would suffer heavily —as they ought to do—if taken out of their present employment. They are inseparable from the whole, and in themselves they are moving and exciting.

There are three high spots dramatically in *The Birthday of the Infanta*. The third and last of them is at the death of the dwarf, the very end of the play; and here the scene subordinates itself; it only envelops the action in a towering, rich shadow, and leaves the moment to the music, whose language best suits its poignant necessity. But the drama of the two others is almost entirely created by the setting. One of these places is where against those iron bars and the hard mountains beyond them, the Princess and her ladies in their citron color, their crimson, blurred saffron, rose and white, gold, silver, and black, sit on the balustrade above the courtyard, and the little hunchback below in his pallor and drab and green reaches up his lean hands toward the dazzling splendor of them. And the other and still more dramatic incident—and more simply achieved—is that earlier moment when the little Princess enters that great door, and stands there under the height of it and at the top of the steps leading down, a figure like a doll in all that relentless magnificence and order, symbol of the tragic puppetry of all life in the midst of time and the world's vastness, her grave and delicate little body borne along in those billowy, great skirts as her heart is borne on the waves of the music.

And, finally, this achievement in the *décor* for *The Birthday of the Infanta*, illustrates remarkably how in the art of the theatre, precisely as in other arts, say music, painting, poetry, the reality must be restated in terms of the art concerned before there is any art at all. It must have the charm of presence and absence, as Pascal said of portraits. An element must be there which was not there before. It must be incredibly translated into something else; it must be the same and not the same, like the moon in water, by a certain nameless difference born anew.

SOPHOCLES' GUEST

THERE is no doubt a young man somewhere who might very well go to see *Œdipus Rex* at one of those classical revivals of the play in Athens. And the brunt of the play's mind on him and the power of Greek thought and life might set up something like a conversion, for a time at least, and divert him into new but yet old and habitable ways.

He is an American youth, grown up in an average town; he has an honest, active life in him and a certain readiness of motion in numerous directions. He is typical but not average. His nerves are keen, his brain alive; and in the midst of him is something that is busy, half troubled, and a little wistful. He has known no society in any large sense, only the unit that the family is—an unsettled unit to be sure nowadays—and a series of parties and entertainments by which people tend to bring themselves more or less together. The natural world he has lived with healthily: excursions, walks, and games, and sometimes with a shy poignancy and dream in his heart at the aspect of nature's beauty and growth and mystery. At college he was not wholly usual, since he studied and read. And he came out of college with what is not to him a satisfactory amount of information, loyalties, concessions, borrowings from others and thwartings of himself. He knows that there is something that he wants more of; what that something is, exactly, remains intense but vague. Despite his father he knows, at least, that he wants to write; he wants to express the life he sees; he sees the swarm and flow of American life, he reads the publicities of the American press about the theatre, and he wants to write plays.

The young man believes that energy and movement will carry him through, and that in these terms he can grapple with life and out of it create an art. And yet, behind this energy and faith in acquisition, he is restless; he drives and wheedles and bites at life. He is hungry for himself. He is perpetually taking himself to pieces without knowing just what is the design into which he is trying to put himself together again.

Without believing anything very clearly this young man is a strong believer. He is not poetic in the traditional sense of the word in English societies; he is for something more active, doubtless, than he conceives poetry to be. He is not poetic, for he is unwilling to let the quietness and lure of romantic meditation take their way with him, or to make his dream a passion. But he is enthusiastic; he thinks that life can be made to express him. He sows himself on life, which is the poet working in him after all.

Of science this young man knows a good deal; he had in college waves and fads of it, mixed in with philosophy and personal fashions in psychology and the social theories of the day. He has still a certain laboratory cockiness about small facts that seem to him incontestably supported by investigations, however small. In religion he has fads likewise, is prepared for anything, the news of a dozen new cults a year. Of the soul's journalism he is a busy and well-posted subscriber. But in general he holds to his father's religion and rebels against it when he chooses; that constitutes his religious activity, so far as one sees it, though he has his mystery there too. And what he knows most about of late years is the science, the psychology and religion of sex. He, along with his fellows, has read both the new and the old books on that subject; they consider themselves experts on it, and are open to every comer, every explanation, disenchantment, or inspiration. Psychoanalysis is the best guide for his raids in such research. In politics he has certain notions of the game. His thoughts are tinged with a suggestive but not dangerous socialism. He has heard much of social service, of universal brotherhood, the outlawry of war, and normalcy, whatever that may be. In con-

ceptions and general ideas he cannot be said to
have laid his ground very spaciously. He has a
vast mixture of theories, points-of-view, creeds,
and systems. Perhaps the most nearly inclusive
idea he has is that of uniformity. Not conformity; he would resent having to conform to any
will or dictum; it is uniformity that he moves
toward; he likes to have men and things one at
bottom and going on from that one into all—
in sum, he likes variety rather than difference.
And yet he does not; and no one knows what
wildness may be in his heart, though the American life around makes the release of it distaste-
ful even to him.

But, whatever else this youth may be, he is
racial in that he is an individualist. He is not
always an individualist in any important sense,
driving individualism into an idea; and not always impetuously an individualist. But he begins obstinately with himself. He is, in some
odd way, his own authority, the editor of himself. He sees heaven with his own eyes, and those
are his feet that tread and define whatever cos-
mic tracks he traverses. He sets out to think for
himself and to take his own where he finds it.
His mind is accordingly a rag-bag. Into it this
notion and that, this thought or system or quota-
tion, is received protestingly or eagerly but always personally, for he mistrusts order or rule
or authority. He has little impulse, so far as he

realizes, toward any but a personal arrangement and outlook on all life and all culture and
thought. But as it leaps here and there his is a
sensitive spirit, somewhat starved by the thin-
ness of the life he has seen, and somewhat hur-
ried and confused by the stream of his country
and era. His wits are alive, and his eyes and
legs wandering and avid.

He goes then to the play, down to the Theatre
of Dionysos, through the lively streets. By some
happy arrangement the play will be given in the
morning, with the bright light of the sun over-
head, the country and the people set forth with
the life of the morning on them. From the lines
of the open theatre the eyes travel to the lines
of the surrounding world, as they are led upward to the sky by the descending light. The
play begins, not perfectly done, of course, not
drilled enough, and not with any complete
knowledge of how Sophocles' Athenians employed the various theatrical mediums, the recitation, the movement, the music, to create the
dramatist's idea. But behind the makeshift and
the imperfections the old forms are shadowed
nevertheless; and what the ancient order of
thought and the ancient quality of beauty were
is still to be discerned.

The play begins. The crowd enters, the people driven by pestilence toward their king and
toward the gods. The prophet comes; a curse is

on the land. Œdipus sets out upon the search that is to be his fate. Jocasta, ill-starred and violent, the woman who is his mother and also his wife, throws herself between Œdipus and this knowledge that will destroy them all. And finally in shame and frenzy Jocasta hangs herself, and Œdipus with the clasps of her robe digs out his eyes. He enters then with that most terrible shudder in all drama; he feels the pain, his voice floats far from him, shame in this world and in the next he feels; all things, even his children, are taken from him, and he goes out to wander alone over the world. And meanwhile the chorus has sung and moved and carried into a wider region the events of the play and the thoughts of the characters. The music of the instruments has widened yet further the whole, giving it a yet more general and essential abstraction, and seeming to spread upon it an aspect of the eternal. The changing lines of the chorus and the actors have rendered less obscure the poet's desire and all his thought; the wind from Salamis, blowing another rhythm into those bright garments, has carried into universal space that flow of movement under the wide light.

The young man sits and sees and hears. All very well and very classical, no doubt, but a man thinks for himself. He has resisted at first. Life, he insists, is not so simple as all this. This story of Œdipus is moulded from without, it stood ready to Sophocles' hand; into this story the characters are fitted, with their several parts to bear and their functions to perform in a general idea. And these characters are not people, they are figures with vast outlines in some yet larger outline. Through them, as through the story, the forces play. This entire arrangement and spectacle, the movements, the acting, the scene, are not actual but as far away as the story is and the figures in it. The young man tells himself that if you simplify life in this fashion you are avoiding its point and problem.

Gradually, nevertheless, something has happened; it is as if the landscape had sunk into him. He begins to have within him the sense of a long, deep vista, a clearness, an impersonal ascent. And at length he walks away in the midst of the crowd, who are discussing the play and the performance of it with such volubility.

Hours pass as he walks about the streets; for, by some persuasion new to his mind, the thoughts he has, however privately, must be carried through to their conclusion publicly. They must be thought among thoroughfares of men, and not in those places that he sees stretching far off into the country, leading their quiet planes in the soft light and under lengthening shadows. He thinks of Leonardo da Vinci's phrase that he has wondered about at home, "how sweet the people's faces in the streets," and for the first time it seems simple and without sentiment to him. How sweet the people's faces that he sees passing by in the streets; how open and gentle life seems in them! And then, as he must do if he is not to be a traitor to his race, he goes back to his own room and closes the door. He sits down by the open window, settles himself, and, in a way that makes us love his kind, he takes stock.

The world, it seems, if we listen to Sophocles and his classical art, consists for us of our ideas as they arise, survive, complete themselves. There are many things that we do not understand in the universe, in life, in ourselves. But we may have a sense of a line, perhaps, of a scope, a continuity. We may not understand anything at all in itself, but we can see its relation to other things in our world of living and ideas. And we can move toward ideas, conceptions, in which many things take their places. We may discover, evolve, and create patterns, images, symbols, conceptions. Is it possible, he begins to ask himself, that some kinds of living are more representative, more inclusive of all life? And would the art, therefore, that expressed such living have a form that might remain significant and seem to include or comment on the rest of life?

The young man hurls himself about; a great

force has taken him. He will never be at home
in this classical world of thought, of art, of life,
he knows; but he knows, too, that he should not
be, since he is an American and not a Greek of
Sophocles' time. Other kinds of art, he knows
very well, are good also; they have each one its
necessity for existence. His brain tells him that
every kind of living must find the expression
closest to it; Strindberg for the life he expresses,
Chekhov for his, Ibsen, D'Annunzio, Bernard
Shaw. And yet he is held; Sophocles has made
an inroad on him.

As for these ideas, these permanent forms
and conceptions within which Sophocles sets his
drama and his comment on living, the young
man reminds himself that in the natural world
around us what survives and reappears is form,
idea, not the dust that goes to the making of every
tree and beast. Nature constantly approximates
finalities, forms within which life may complete
and express itself forever. Why not likewise in
the realm of human living and thought?

As he sits there brooding he is suddenly dis-
armed by recognizing what has been the direction of late that he himself and his friends have
taken when in their criticism of life they draw on
science. He remembers how often one said these
days that such and such a man was in such and
such a class physiologically, biologically or what
not, and that this explained and concluded him.

He remembers how much the theories of punishment and crime, of prisons and schools, turn nowadays not on individuals in themselves so much as on the characteristics and forces that make them what they are and make them act as they do. Science and visitation of forces; gods, then, we may as well call them gods and let the Greeks have it their way. In the human body the visitation and shock of universal elements! We may have the will to suppress and repress and control; but the forces come; if at no other time, they possess our dreams, gods coming in dreams to men! The young man's father would have denied that; such a point of view would have insulted character, will, morality and Queen Victoria. Not so with the young man and his friends; they were ready to receive the light of almost any theory. What would his father think when he heard that time, motion and space cannot be absolute, since their measurement is relative to the observer? Or that the ether we had been filling the universe with had never existed at all? And here in Greek the same kind of thinking went on, free and luminous. But it moved not so much toward relaxations and the loosening of standards as toward outlines, forms, a sense of ideas into which contributing details took their relative place.

It was like those charts of mariners that lead to conceived and desired ends, to harbors and over tracks that have been plotted out. Under these lines of purpose and direction lies the sea, a ceaseless, ungoverned passion of energy and eternal power, an unfathomed and inexhaustible mystery of being, a boundless vitality and danger. But the chart remains and man's navigation may be informed by it. There are ports foreseen and attainable for the voyage that he must make, no matter what his will is or the weariness and perplexity of his heart.

The art, or the thinking, that follows such a conception is by its own nature driven to find its charts and possible ways. It plots out, above the immense and inexhaustible sources of human nature and living, an order, a plan, a course in art that will bring us to rational and sweet harbors, and into ports and havens from which we may look out over the ocean with some consolation of understanding. A man's life, then, under this Greek scheme, moves perpetually through the expression and the discipline of it toward a large and grave and foreseen outline, a beautiful and persuasive design. Under this Greek scheme a man respects in art lucidity and consummate statement and the recreative power of clear light; he doubts the virtue of that which skilful confusion or poignant chaos may stumble upon. To him art must be passionate and universal, but the born heir of a divine and tranquil nature.

Suddenly his American uniformity appears to be a small thing. It is only a poor version of conformity after all. That a race of men should contemplate the same ideas—love, justice, say—with a view toward the progress, clarity, and completion of them, might be a fine thing. That all men should be expected to agree to certain conceptions or applications of these ideas—love, justice, say—is stupid, narrow and mediocre. To the young man sitting there at his Athens window this thought is a shock. He begins to ask himself if belief is merely personal, stubborn, insistent. His body does not live only by what it attacks, bites, adopts, chews up, makes it own. It lives also by what rests on no personal determination at all, and by the healthful light, the respiration of his lungs, and the beating of his heart that sends the blood—whose hidden crimson is so magnificent—through his veins. How foolish it would be, he starts suddenly and decides, to set up a dogma, a belief about the beating of his heart!

The race behind this classic art of Greece, the young man reflects, was at home in the world. But it was not at home in the same way that he had been, restlessly optimistic, confident that things could be made to work. There may be something in that, if you will; but after Sophocles it seems only an adolescent courage and evasion. This at-homeness of the Greeks arose from other things, from a lively and keen-eyed response to the world and observation of it, and a sense of *fatalità*, as the Italians call it—fatality, though that is too depressing a word for it—destiny, though that word is too dark. As for the young man, he understands from his heritage of religious philosophy a kind of mysticism, a resignation before the will of God, a kind of Christian, Oriental, mediæval abnegation of self. But he sees that this Greek fatality of Sophocles' is an idea arising from an experience with the universe that has confronted the universe with the human mind and has perceived what appear to be processes working in their due courses and including man with them.

The young man thinks of the life he has known in America. That life, he knows, has simplified itself and lost much of an old, long world-culture. The wholesale methods by which ideas are sent broadcast into men's minds, and the reduction of all ideas to a popular accessibility and simplicity, what do they promise for American life? Is it moving toward a certain large outline? Something more single? The beginning of a new myth, more elemental, final, universal? But for such ends to attain to any importance or significance there would have to be not merely a simplification of life and popular culture that is directed toward less complexity; it must also be directed toward essentials. Intelligence, effort, time, would be needed for that, if it is ever to come. His thought travels to the theatre. How far are we tired of photography, of accidental living, of a false plausibility that satisfies the comfortable and commonplace? Do we move toward larger ideas in our theatre, however simple and lacking in finality our statement of them might be?

But when all else is said and done, there is one thing in Sophocles that sticks in the young man's craw; he will not admit the characters as they are in this Greek drama. Men to him are individuals, each with his peculiar ways, his personal traits, his twists and turns; our whole racial tradition of an individual starts with these private details. Sophocles' people, he objects obstinately within himself, are not persons at all, this so-called Œdipus and Jocasta and Creon. They, too, are only types, outlines, they move in forms, they are created of only ideal substance. According to this classical art, he discerns, the centre of a man is universal, not private. Man takes his glory from all glory, he embodies rather than evolves it. Man is most himself, Sophocles says, when he is most universal; universal not by some mystical ecstasy and sense of entrance into the heart of God, as the youth in his quieter hours has thought or read in the saints, but by

some completion in himself of ideas, of enduring conceptions, and of what has been profoundly continuous in human experience.

It was the shock of all such in men's minds,
and especially in the minds of the great poets,
that drove into being those vast images—Oedipus, Agamemnon, Electra, Orestes, Antigone
and the rest—to fill our thoughts and, as Aeschy-
lus said of Prometheus, to make men cease from
contemplating death.

As for our young man he does not move, but
sits brooding on those great tragic personages;
they do not limit him; in them he walks and finds
himself, the terror and magnificence of what a
man is; and he is not one but all of them. It is
as if in some heroic music his own heart heard
its beating. And now he thinks of his walk in
Athens yesterday. He had gone down along the
Ilyssus and then to the Eleusis road. Along that
road, as he passed the hill where once stood
Oedipus' Kolonos there came a goatherd leading
his beasts and playing a shepherd's pipe. The
pipe rose like a deathless voice clearly toward
the clear night.

In the wood at home, the young man remembers, his thoughts had not been anywhere in
particular, but he had found his spirits rested
and soothed. He had come home from those
walks in many moods, muddled, lifted, desperate
with the shadow of vague yearning. He had felt

in his heart a shy tenderness, and even among his companions afterward a kind of blunt lyricism. Sometimes he had felt himself religious: the mystery of the universe had seemed to minister to him. He wondered now about that religion and about his preoccupation at times with what he had been taught was religion; how much of it was merely insistent details in egotism?

Along that clear road through the burnt, harsh, yellow and violet land, with the rocks, he had gone yesterday and had returned at length through the teeming streets to his own room. About all this there had been a sense first of all of shapes and spaces, and of the eye recognizing its own judgement and power and delight. He had felt a sense of permanency not within himself, but in that part of himself that lived in those forms and qualities that appeared in the world around him. He sits there by his window looking out on the mountains, Lykabettos and the long slopes of Pentelicos and the country around. The late sun lies yellow on them; on the walls of the town; the Bay of Salamis grows darker and bluer. And sitting there he sees the great night come on. Over the sad land he sees the stars rise; and tonight at least, watching them in the clear heavens and the forms they take, he thinks not on the mystery but on the pattern of his soul.